little kitchen

little kitchen

40 Delicious and Simple Things That Children Can Really Make

Sabrina Parrini

Photography by Jacqui Melville

Skyhorse Publishing

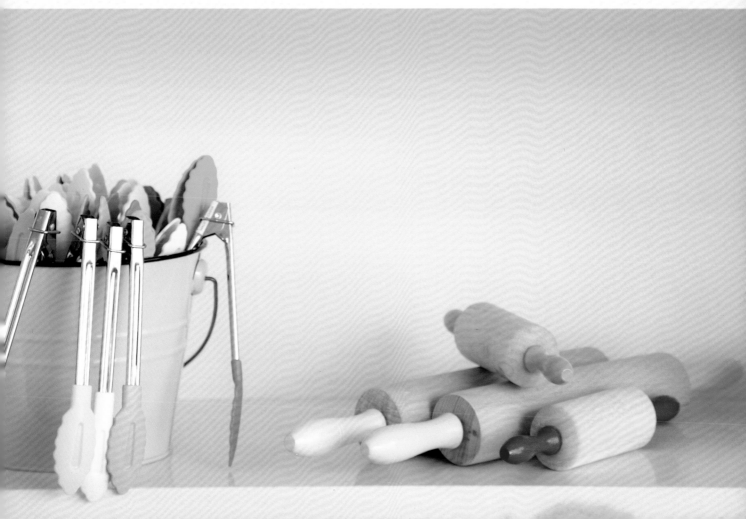

Skyhorse Publishing books may be purchased in bulk at special discounts for sales promotion, corporate gifts, fund-raising, or educational purposes. Special editions can also be created to specifications. For details, contact the Special Sales Department, Skyhorse Publishing, 307 West 36th Street, 11th Floor, New York, NY 10018 or info@skyhorsepublishing.com.

www.skyhorsepublishing.com

10 9 8 7 6 5 4 3 2

Library of Congress Cataloging-in-Publication Data

Parrini, Sabrina.
  Little kitchen : 40 delicious and simple things that children can really make / Sabrina Parrini.
      p. cm.
  ISBN 978-1-61608-188-1 (pbk. : alk. paper)
  1. Cooking--Juvenile literature. 2. Cookbooks. I. Title.
  TX652.5.P3723 2010
  641.5'123--dc22
                              2010024292

Printed in China

Edited by Lucy Rushbrooke
Designed by Trisha Garner
Typesetting by Pauline Haas
Photography by Jacqui Melville
Color reproduction by Splitting Image Color Studio

Thanks to the following for their generosity in supplying props for the book: The Essential Ingredient, Market Import, and Meet Me at Mikes.

Many thanks also go to Demi, Ella, Georgia, Holly, Lily, Minna, Peri, Shaini, and Tess for their help.

While this book aims to accurately describe what steps a child should be able to perform reasonably independently when cooking, a supervising adult must be present at all times. An adult should always use good judgement about a child's capabilities and read the Safety First information on page xvi before attempting any of the recipes.

The author and the publishers take no responsibility for any injury caused while cooking a recipe from this book. Nor are they responsible for any allergic reactions that may eventuate as a result of using this cookbook. It is the supervising adult's sole responsibility to ensure a child who has allergies doesn't cook a recipe that is inappropriate.

To my dear mum, Maria,
my first and best cookery teacher

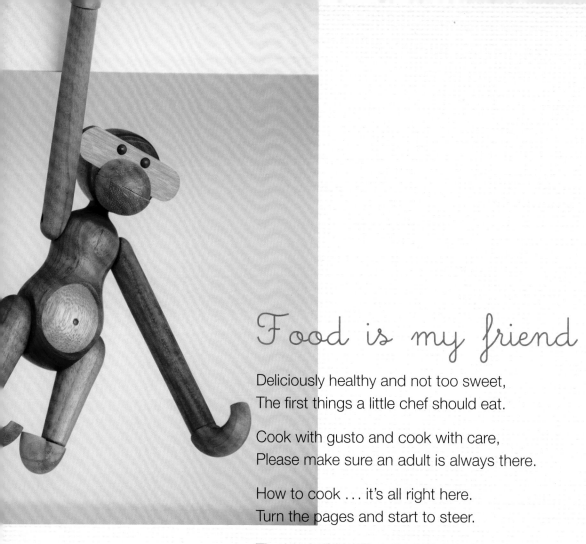

Food is my friend

Deliciously healthy and not too sweet,
The first things a little chef should eat.

Cook with gusto and cook with care,
Please make sure an adult is always there.

How to cook … it's all right here.
Turn the pages and start to steer.

The land of food now awaits you.
So, happy cooking all the year through!

CONTENTS

Dear little chefs,

My family is Italian. And Italians love food. They love shopping for it, cooking it, and eating it.

You don't need to be Italian to love preparing and enjoying food though. No matter where you come from, however old you are, or whatever you look like, food is an important part of everyone's life. Good food keeps us happy, healthy, and strong.

Because of this, it's really important to learn how to cook—and more importantly, how to cook well. By cooking well, I mean knowing how to cook real food. Real food means meals that you can prepare using whole, recognizable ingredients, not those that come in powdered form from a packet off the supermarket shelf.

By cooking from this book, you'll soon get to know how to look after yourself properly and also how to care for those around you. Remember (as one of my favorite authors once said), nothing says, "I like you" better than a delicious meal.

By holding this book in your hands, you're about to make a new friend.

Food is my friend ... let's make it yours too!

Happy cooking and eating!

Sabrina

Sabrina

P.S. You'll find lots of useful information about ingredients and equipment in the pages that follow, but above all, before you start cooking, make sure that you AND a grown-up read the Safety First information on page xvi.

Dear parents,

The chances are that if you are reading this book you already know the reasons why it's so important for children to learn about cooking. So this letter is not about reiterating what you already know. Instead it contains a few suggestions about the ways in which you can make cooking a happy experience for your little chefs—and for you!

To be honest, it takes time and patience to let young children into your kitchen. It is often quicker and easier to do things yourself. But if you take the time to encourage children to cook from an early age there are plenty of rewards for parents and carers in the long run. Not only do children learn important life skills in the kitchen, but as they get older, they will be able (and willing) to take over a lot of the meal preparation at home!

For children to gain confidence and the necessary skills, you will probably need to set some ground rules. Mostly, these are common sense, and are to do with safety. For this reason, it is vitally important that you AND your child read the Safety First information on page xvi. And remember that children learn a lot of their own habits from observing grown-ups, so try to adopt good kitchen behavior yourself. Wash your own hands before touching food, tie long hair back, wear an apron, and pull up long sleeves. And try not to do things in the kitchen that you wouldn't want your children to do—such as dipping questionably clean fingers into a dish to taste it!

I'd love you to read as much of the information contained in the first part of this book as you can. And encourage your children to read this information with you—even though they will probably want to jump straight into the fun cooking part!

Plan to cook when you have plenty of time, so you don't feel rushed and everyone can enjoy the experience. It's a good idea to cook on weekends or during school vacation, instead of on a school day when you may be pressed for time, tired, or stressed. In my experience, it's when you try to rush things that things go wrong and safety can be compromised.

Read the recipe through with your children, from beginning to end, before you start, so that you know what you are doing. Then assemble all the ingredients and equipment that you need.

The recipes in this book are intended for children aged six years and up. Some are fairly simple, while others are more complex and will even challenge young adults. Decide which parts of the recipe your own children can manage safely, then work through things together.

While all the recipes clearly indicate where full adult supervision is essential from a safety perspective, they are also designed to give children as broad an experience of cooking as possible. So I encourage you to allow them to do as much as possible, unaided. Children thrive on independence, so even if they are slow or messy, or not doing a task as "well" as you could, give them the space and freedom to learn. Research has found that cooking with children from a young age can positively affect their mental and emotional well-being.

While some of the fun of cooking is knowing when and how to improvise, I strongly recommend that you and your little chefs start by following a recipe to the letter. Young children, in particular, need clarity and direction in the kitchen to achieve success. As a child gets older and becomes more adept, you can introduce the concepts of ingredient substitution and food matching.

Finally, you may think that the recipes in this book look longer than recipes in other children's cookbooks. This is partly because I am assuming little prior experience, so each step is clearly explained in detail for your little chef to follow. But mainly it is because the recipes in the *Little Kitchen* cookbook are proper recipes—not just cookies, cakes, and snacks—so that your children can learn how to cook proper meals.

I hope that together you will create lots of happy shared memories in the kitchen—and that your whole family will enjoy the delicious results!

I wish you a happy time in the kitchen!

Sabrina

Sabrina

Safety first

Although cooking is great fun, it is important to remember that some things in the kitchen can be dangerous if you are not careful. For this reason it is very important to have an adult stay in the kitchen with you the whole time you are cooking.

Knives and sharp equipment

Knives, peelers, graters, and food processors are sharp, so when they are called for in a recipe, I recommend that a grown-up should always be close by to help. Very small children may not be experienced or big enough to use knives safely, in which case an adult should do what is required themselves.

Sharp knives are safer than blunt knives because you don't need to use as much pressure to cut with them. When you use less pressure, you are less likely to slip and cut yourself.

Don't put a knife—or anything sharp—into a sink of water for washing where it can't be seen. If someone doesn't know it is there, they might cut themselves.

Oven and stovetop

Ovens and stovetops get very hot so I recommend that a grown-up should always be present when they are in use. Ask a grown-up to help you turn the heat on and off and to adjust the temperature to the correct level.

When using the oven, remember to arrange the racks in the right place BEFORE you turn it on. In general the middle rack is the best spot for cooking because it allows the hot air to move all around your dish and cook the food evenly.

Stand back when the oven door is being opened as the hot steam can burn. Both grown-ups and children should use oven mitts when moving things in and out of the oven. Ideally they should be long enough to cover your forearms—and please make sure they are the right size for your hands: small mitts for small hands.

When cooking on the stovetop, always ask a grown-up to turn the heat on and to adjust it to the correct temperaure. Either you or an adult MUST hold the handle steady when stirring something in a pan on the stovetop. Always wear oven mitts when working near a stovetop or with hot ingredients.

Turn the handles of pots and pans so they face to the back or side of the stove. Handles poking out could cause an accident if someone accidentally knocks them. Never leave them unattended and always remember to turn the heat off when you are finished.

Always use a timer, so you don't overcook or burn anything; it's easy to forget how long something has been cooking! Never leave the kitchen when you have something on the stovetop as it may burn or catch on fire.

Spills

Always clean up spills right away. Spills on the floor make it slippery and you might slip and fall over. Wipe up with paper towels and once you've cleaned up, tell everyone else to be careful of the wet floor.

Allergies

If you don't already know, check with your parents or a grown-up to find out if you are allergic to any foods. If you are, ALWAYS tell the adult you are cooking with before you start. They might not know or they might have forgotten. Make sure you both check the recipe carefully to make sure it doesn't use any ingredients you can't have. If you are unsure about something, it's safer to choose another recipe instead.

Food safety

It's important to follow some simple hygiene rules when cooking so that no one gets sick! If you are cooking with both raw meats and vegetables, make sure you use two separate chopping boards and never use the same knife to chop vegetables after you've cut up meat. This is because raw meats sometimes have bacteria in them (that are killed by the cooking process) that you don't want to end up on your veggies!

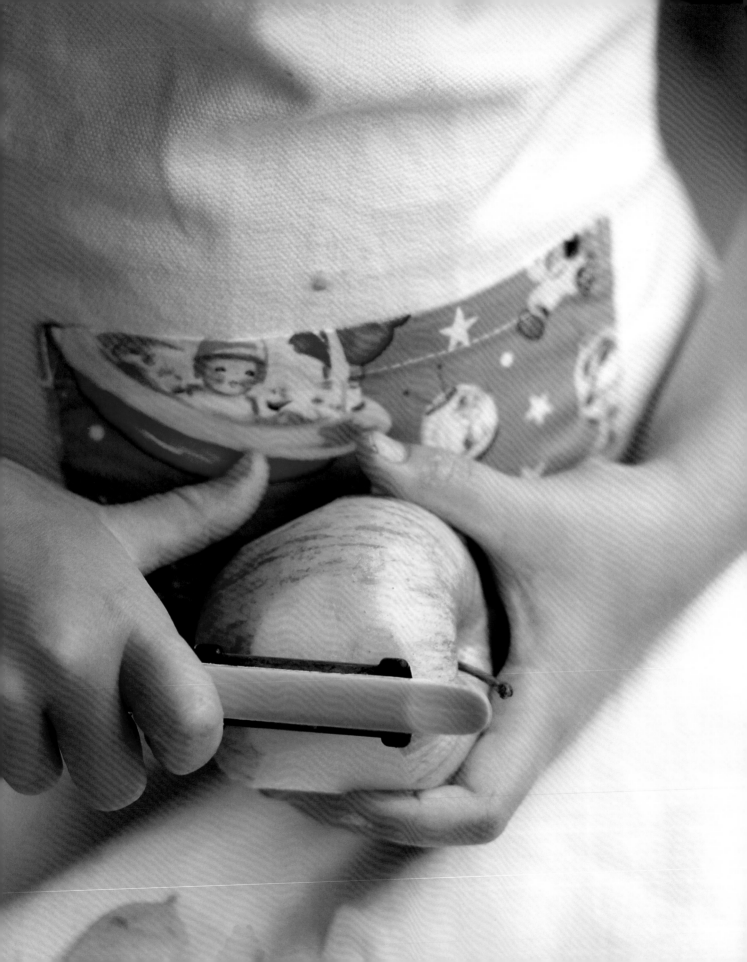

Ingredients

Little Kitchen is all about helping children understand that if you start off with good-quality ingredients you'll end up with good-quality—and much tastier—food. In my classes I've seen the fun that children have preparing recipes from scratch. They find it so much more satisfying than just opening packets of ready-mix or pre-prepared foods. That's why I like to use "proper" food as much as possible, and it's why I keep packets and tins (with their added preservatives and artificial colorings and flavorings) to a minimum.

Some families have their own vegetable gardens or herb gardens, which really allow children to experience the link between the garden and the table. Otherwise, I try to encourage people to buy and cook fruits and vegetables when they are in season. The produce will taste better and will be more nutritious.

Although *Little Kitchen* focuses on healthy and wholesome food, we also believe that eating is about balance. That means we do sometimes use sugar, butter, cream, and cheese in our recipes. You could say we're into being healthy, but without taking it to extremes.

Here are some recommendations about ingredients for the recipes in this book:

* Onions are brown onions.

* Milk is whole milk.

* Cream is heavy-whipping (low-fat cream does not whip).

* Meat is free-range and lean.

* Mayonnaise is Greek-style.

* Canned tuna is preserved in oil and without added flavorings.

* Eggs are 2 oz, free-range, and should be brought to room temperature before cooking.

* Pepper is black pepper, finely ground.

* Pasta and risotto rice: I've tried cooking with the cheapest and the most expensive pastas and risotto rice to see if there is any difference other than price. All I can say is if you purchase the cheapest product it will be more likely to break apart during the cooking. It's better to invest a few more dollars and buy a quality brand, as the result will be more appetizing.

* I like to use vanilla-bean paste, but you can substitute the same amount of vanilla extract if you prefer.

* Stock is homemade if possible as the flavor is so much nicer.

Equipment

For each recipe you'll find a list of the equipment that you will need for preparing the ingredients.

Knives and chopping boards

Use a bigger knife for bigger ingredients and a smaller knife for smaller ingredients. Serrated knifes are best for slicing bread. Remember that all knives should be kept sharp as blunt knives are more dangerous. (See page xvi for safety information.)

Always use a chopping board when you are using a knife so that you don't scratch the kitchen counter or tabletop. It is important that the board doesn't slip around on the counter, so either use one that has a non-slip rubber base or rubber feet, or place a damp tea towel beneath the board to keep it steady. A bigger board is better, as you have more room to work on.

Use two chopping boards if you need to prepare meat and vegetables in the same recipe.

Scissors

Scissors are ideal for snipping herbs. Use small, child-safe scissors when possible.

Graters and peelers

Little chefs will find a box grater is easiest for grating and zesting. Conical graters and microplane zesters may be suitable for older children, but they do require a little more dexterity, because of their shape and the angle at which you need to hold the food. Try to use a grater that has a rubber handle on it and a non-slip rubber base to prevent accidents occurring due to loss of steadiness.

It takes a bit of practice to use a peeler. Try to hold food steady on a chopping board and peel in long smooth movements, rather than little bits at a time.

Measuring jugs, measuring cups, measuring spoons

Although sometimes you will have to weigh an ingredient using kitchen scales, wherever possible, I've suggested using measuring jugs, cups, and spoons to measure ingredients. Don't use regular cups and spoons because they come in all sorts of different shapes and sizes, which means they won't be accurate.

Jugs are for measuring liquids, like milk and stock. To measure accurately, place the jug on the work surface and measure the ingredient to the marked line—not over or under it.

Cups are for measuring solid ingredients, like rice or flour. To measure accurately, heap the ingredient up high, then use a spatula to smooth over the top and make it level.

Spoons are for measuring smaller amounts of liquids or solids, such as honey or milk, baking powder or sugar. To measure accurately, heap the ingredient up high, then use a spatula to smooth over the top to make it level.

Mixing bowls

I recommend you have several different-sized mixing bowls—small, medium, and large—to match the quantity of ingredients. Metal or plastic bowls are ideal as they are light and won't break if you drop them. Shallow bowls make mixing easier for children. When mixing in a bowl, use one hand to hold it steady on the counter and one hand to mix.

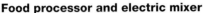

Food processor and electric mixer

Both these machines make kitchen work easier! Food processors are great for chopping ingredients quickly or turning them into a paste. Sometimes you have to scrape the ingredients down from the sides of the bowl so they mix in properly. Always make sure a grown-up puts in and removes the sharp blade and that they help you turn the machine on and off.

Electric mixers make cakes and cookies easy. A grown-up should help you fit the correct attachment to the machine, help you set the correct speed, and watch while you use it. A k-beater is used for beating, while a whisk is used to whip cream or egg whites.

Saucepans

I use a set of different-sized saucepans with a spout for easy pouring. Smaller saucepans are perfect for melting butter or chocolate or cooking smaller quantities. Use a large saucepan for cooking soup, pasta, or rice. Saucepans should have a tight-fitting lid and a handle that won't get hot when you are cooking.

Frying pans

As the name suggests, these are for frying ingredients—often in a little bit of oil or butter. Non-stick pans are great because you can fry without oil and they are very easy to clean. Use a deeper pan for deep-frying. Some ingredients, such as nuts and spices, are dry-roasted without oil. Make sure your frying pans have a handle that won't get hot when you are cooking.

Colanders

These are used to drain boiled vegetables and pasta. Always ask a grown-up to help you and be careful to stand away from the hot steam. The safest way to drain hot items is to place the colander in the sink and pour the hot contents in.

Sieves and sifters

These have a fine mesh and are used to sift flour, confectioners sugar, or cocoa to remove any lumps. They are often used when making cakes or batters, to ensure the mixture is smooth and light.

Oven

At Little Kitchen we use a fan-forced electric oven, and this is what we used to test the recipes in this book. Generally, fan-forced ovens cook faster than other ovens so you might need to adjust cooking temperatures and times if you have a conventional oven. Make sure you read the Safety First information on page xvi for more information about using ovens.

Cookie sheets, baking pans, and muffin trays

Cookie sheets are metal trays for cooking things in the oven. Some are deep and are used for roasting meat. Shallow sheets are used for cooking things like cookies. Often, cookie sheets will need to be greased before use to stop food sticking. Use a piece of scrunched-up baking paper to rub the tray all over with a little butter or oil.

Baking pans and muffin trays come in different shapes and sizes. Make sure you use the correct size for the recipe you are preparing and grease or line it with baking paper, according to the instructions.

Baking dishes and ovenproof dishes

These are dishes that are able to be used in the oven without breaking. They are used for bakes, slices, casseroles, and pies.

Wire racks

These are essential for cooling cakes or cookies after they come out of the oven.

Utensils

Spoons can be wooden or metal and are used for stirring. In general, I recommend using spoons with long handles when stirring something in a pan on the stovetop to keep hands well away from hot contents. Slotted spoons are useful for lifting solid ingredients, such as gnocchi, out of a liquid.

Tongs are perfect for moving things around in a pan or on the barbecue.

Whisks are used when you want to remove lumps to make a smooth sauce, or when you want to incorporate some air into ingredients such as cream or egg whites.

Spatulas and **palette knives** are perfect for scraping out bowls or for spreading fillings or icings onto cakes.

Egg flips are not just for eggs. They are useful for turning all sorts of things over in pans or for lifting them out.

Ladles are perfect for serving soups and stews as they hold more than spoons.

Cookie cutters come in all sorts of shapes and sizes and are great for making cookies or shortcakes.

Pastry brushes are used to brush pastry with melted butter, egg, or milk before baking, so that it turns golden and shiny. A brush can also be used to marinate meat before cooking.

Plastic wrap comes in rolls and is used to wrap and seal food to stop it from drying out in the air.

Paper towel is absorbent paper that is used for mopping up spills in the kitchen or for draining food that has been fried.

Baking paper is often lightly coated in silicon and is used to line cookie sheets and baking pans so that cookies or cakes won't stick.

Top tips for little chefs

Read the recipe through from beginning to end before you start, and ask an adult to explain anything you don't understand.

Wash your hands well with warm soapy water before you begin. Wear an apron and make sure your sleeves are properly rolled up. If you have long hair, tie it back.

Lay out all your ingredients and equipment on the kitchen counter before you begin cooking. This is what chefs call *"mise en place"* which means "to put things in place" in French. It's the best way of knowing you have everything you need so you don't find out halfway through a recipe that your brother has just used up all the milk!

Wash and dry all fruit and vegetables before starting.

If you know you're going to cook something the next day that uses eggs or butter, take them out of the fridge the night before (or the morning of cooking if it's very hot weather!) and place them on the kitchen counter to come to room temperature.

Preheat the oven so that it comes to the correct temperature BEFORE you put something inside to cook.

Keep the oven door closed the whole time you are cooking—especially if you're baking a cake or soufflé. Opening the door lets out a lot of heat and it may spoil a recipe.

Set a timer to remind you when something has finished cooking—it's very easy to forget.

Taste things as you go along (using a spoon, not your finger). That way you know if you need to adjust the seasoning or sweetness of a dish before you get to the end.

Clean up as you go along so you don't have a huge pile of washing up to do when you've finished cooking. And don't leave your mess for someone else to clean up. Mop up spills right away to keep your work area clean and tidy. Use a sponge to wipe down the kitchen work surface and if you spill anything on the floor, clean it up with paper towels that you can throw away.

When you serve food try to make it look attractive on the plate! Many people believe that we "eat" with our eyes, as well as with our mouths, so presentation is important.

Most importantly, remember that cooking takes time. Plan to cook when you have plenty of time so you don't feel rushed and can enjoy it. Although cooking is lots of fun, it's still important to concentrate on what you are doing. If you wander in and out of the kitchen and try to do other things at the same time, you might miss important steps and information and your recipe might not turn out right. Eating and sharing delicious food is your reward for all the effort!

Tuna pinwheels

This recipe was inspired by a tuna dip that my mum taught me to make when I was little. If you're feeling adventurous, you might like to add a teaspoon of Madras curry powder to the tuna filling to spice it up.

* Use a rolling pin to flatten each slice of bread.

* **Ask a grown-up** to help you put the onion into a food processor and blitz it to a paste. Once the grown-up has removed the blade from the processor, scrape the paste into a large mixing bowl.

* Place the drained tuna into the bowl and use a fork to break it up into small pieces. Add the cream cheese and mix it together well. Use the scissors to snip the chives into the bowl.

* Use a small palette knife to thickly spread the mixture onto each slice of bread, trying not to go over the edges. Starting at one edge, carefully roll the bread up tightly like a Swiss roll. Place the rolls onto a chopping board with the seam underneath.

* **Ask a grown-up** to help you wrap the rolls tightly in plastic wrap. Twist the ends of the plastic wrap to keep them secure and place them in the fridge to chill for 1–2 hours.

* Take the rolls out of the fridge and remove the plastic wrap. **Ask a grown-up** to help you cut the rolls into about ⅓ in slices and arrange them on a large serving platter.

* *Makes approximately 30 pinwheels*

Ingredients you'll need

6 slices of square whole wheat bread, crusts removed

1 small onion, roughly chopped

1 x 3⅓ oz can of tuna in olive oil, drained

14½ oz cream cheese, softened

9 chives

Equipment you'll need

sharp knife and chopping board

fork

rolling pin

food processor

large mixing bowl

scissors

small palette knife

toaster

plastic wrap

Carrot and zucchini slice

When I was a kindergarten teacher this was one of the most popular dishes on the lunch menu. I know you'll love it too!

Ingredients you'll need

1 teaspoon olive oil for greasing
1 large onion, roughly chopped
¼ cup olive oil
4 small zucchini, grated
3 medium carrots, peeled and grated
1½ cups grated cheddar cheese
½ teaspoon salt
2 pinches of pepper
4 eggs, well beaten
1½ cups self-rising flour

Equipment you'll need

measuring spoons

sharp knife and chopping board

food processor

peeler

measuring cups

mixing bowl

grater

loaf tin

metal skewer

cake slice or egg flip

* **Ask a grown-up** to help you preheat the oven to 350°F. Lightly grease the baking dish.

* **Ask a grown-up** to help you put the onion into a food processor and blitz it to a paste. Once the grown-up has removed the blade from the processor, scrape the paste into a mixing bowl. Add the olive oil and stir it in well.

* Add the grated zucchini, carrots, and cheese to the onion. Add the salt and pepper to the beaten eggs and stir it into the vegetables. Add the flour to the mixture a little bit at a time, stirring it in well as you go.

* **Ask a grown-up** to help you scoop the mixture into the loaf tin. Smooth out the surface so it is even. **Ask a grown-up** to put the loaf tin into the oven and cook for about 45 minutes or until golden brown and cooked through. To test if it is cooked, carefully insert a metal skewer into the middle of the slice; if it comes out clean, the slice is cooked.

* **Ask a grown-up** to remove the loaf tin from the oven and cut the slice into 12 pieces.

* Lift the squares onto a plate using a cake slice or egg flip and serve it with a fresh garden salad and a little dish of tomato sauce or tomato chutney.

* *Makes 12 medium slices*

Minestrone

This is one of my favorite soups and you can use all kinds of vegetables depending on the season. There is quite a lot of preparation to be done, which you can mostly do yourself, as long as there is an adult to help.

* **Ask a grown-up** to help you put the onion and garlic into a food processor and blitz them to a paste. Once the grown-up has removed the blade from the processor, scrape the paste into a small bowl.

* Measure the oil into a large saucepan and **ask a grown-up** to heat it over a low–medium heat. Add the onion and garlic paste and fry until golden, stirring from time to time.

* Add all the vegetables to the saucepan, as well as the canned beans. Crumble in the boullion cube and add the salt and pepper. Pour in the cold water and stir well, then cover with a lid.

* Bring the soup to a boil, then lower the heat and simmer for 1 hour and 15 minutes. Check the water level every now and then and add a little bit more if it seems to be getting low.

* When ready to serve, divide the cooked pasta shapes between 6 bowls. **Ask a grown-up** to ladle the soup on and serve right away.

* *Makes 6 big servings*

Ingredients you'll need

1 large onion, roughly chopped
2 garlic cloves, roughly chopped
2 tablespoons 2 teaspoons olive oil
2 small carrots, peeled and grated
2 small zucchini, grated
1 stick of celery, finely chopped
1 cob of corn, kernels removed
½ x 14 oz can of chopped tomatoes
2 stalks of silverbeet, stems removed and leaves finely shredded
2 cups baby spinach, stems removed
2 cups shelled peas
1 medium potato, peeled and diced into ⅓ in cubes
1 x 15 oz can of beans (borlotti, butter, or kidney beans are all fine), drained and well rinsed
1 vegetable boullion cube
1½ teaspoons salt
3 pinches of pepper
6¼ cups cold water
1¼ cups small pasta shapes, cooked "al dente" *

* "Al dente" means "tender to the bite" in Italian. "Al dente" pasta feels soft when you bite it but is still firm and holds its shape.

Equipment you'll need

sharp knife and chopping board

grater

wooden spoon

food processor

peeler

measuring jug, measuring cups, and measuring spoons

ladle

mixing bowl

large saucepan or stockpot with a lid

Leek and potato potpies

Potatoes and leeks are both in season in autumn and winter and together they make a really tasty filling for a pie.

Ingredients you'll need

1 large onion, roughly chopped
2 garlic cloves, roughly chopped
2 leeks
4 tablespoons olive oil
2½ lbs large floury potatoes, peeled and cut into rough ¾ in cubes
1 teaspoon dried thyme
1¾ cups water
1 chicken or vegetable boullion cube
1½ teaspoons salt
3 pinches of black pepper
2 tablespoons 2 teaspoons all-purpose flour
2 sheets of store-bought puff pastry
4 tablespoons sour cream
1 egg, well beaten

Equipment you'll need

mixing bowl

sharp knife and chopping board

pastry brush

food processor

wooden spoon

peeler

measuring jug

large saucepan with a lid

measuring spoons

2⅓ × 4⅓ in small ovenproof bowls

small cookie cutters

* **Ask a grown-up** to help you preheat the oven to 320°F.

* **Ask a grown-up** to help you put the onion and garlic into a food processor and blitz them to a paste. Once the grown-up has removed the blade from the processor, scrape the paste into a small bowl.

* Cut the hairy ends and the dark green top parts off the leeks and discard them. Slice the leeks in half lengthwise and wash them very well to remove any dirt. Slice them thinly crosswise (into semicircle shapes).

* Measure the oil into a large saucepan and **ask a grown-up** to help you heat it over a medium heat. Scoop in the onion paste and fry it for 1 minute, stirring every now and then. Add the sliced leeks, potato cubes, and thyme. Crumble in the boullion cube and add the salt and pepper. Pour in the cold water and stir well, then cover with a lid and simmer for 30 minutes, or until the potatoes are cooked and most of the liquid has evaporated. Stir every now and then.

* While the vegetables are cooking, shake the flour out onto a work surface and lay out the sheets of puff pastry. Use one of the ovenproof bowls to cut out 6 pastry circles. You should be able to get 4 circles from 1 sheet of pastry so there should be lots of pastry left over.

* Use the cookie cutter to cut out 6 shapes from the leftover pastry to go on top of the pies as decoration.

* When the vegetable filling is cooked, **ask a grown-up** to help you remove it from the heat and let it cool for around 5 minutes. Add the sour cream to the mix and stir it in very quickly so it doesn't curdle. Taste the mixture carefully (**ask a grown-up** to check that it has cooled enough so you don't burn your mouth) and add a bit more salt or pepper if you think it needs it.

* Spoon the mixture into the 6 ovenproof bowls and sit a pastry round on top of each bowl. Decorate with a cut-out pastry shape and brush all over the surface with the beaten egg.

* **Ask a grown-up** to help you put the pies into the oven and bake them for 20 minutes until the pastry is golden.

* **Ask a grown-up** to help you take the pies out of the oven and serve them with a salad or with your favorite seasonal vegetables.

* *Makes 6 small pies*

Fried rice

Fried rice is one of the most popular Asian dishes. I like to serve it in noodle boxes, which are available from party stores. If you like bacon, add a cup of crispy bacon bits when heating the ingredients at the end.

* Measure 3 tablespoons of the sesame oil into a wok. **Ask a grown-up** to help you heat the wok over a medium heat. Add the carrots, zucchini, and scallions and carefully stir them around in the wok so they don't stick. Cook the vegetables for around 15 minutes, or until they have completely softened, stirring them from time to time. **Ask a grown-up** to scoop them into a large mixing bowl.

* Measure out another tablespoon of oil and **ask a grown-up** to add it to the hot wok. Make sure you stand back from the stove in case the oil splatters. **Ask a grown-up** to swirl the oil around in the wok, before adding half of the beaten egg. Quickly swirl the egg around the wok so that it looks like a thin, round pancake. Cook the pancake for 1–2 minutes then flip it over to cook on the other side. When cooked, **ask a grown-up** to carefully slide the pancake onto a chopping board. Repeat with the remaining oil and egg.

* When the pancakes have cooled slightly, roll them into thin "sausages" and **ask a grown-up** to help you slice them thinly so they look like little swirls.

* **Ask a grown-up** to heat the wok again over a medium heat and then to add the rice and vegetables. The bacon should be added now as well, if you are using it. Mix all the ingredients together well, and cook until piping hot.

* To serve, measure 1 cup of fried rice into each noodle box or onto plates. Top with some of the sliced pancake and a little soy sauce. For fun, eat with a bamboo fork or chopsticks!

* *Makes 4 big servings*

Ingredients you'll need

5 tablespoons 1 teaspoon sesame oil
3 small carrots, peeled and grated
3 small zucchini, grated
3 scallions, thinly sliced
3 eggs, well beaten
3 cups cooked, cooled jasmine rice
  (1 cup uncooked)
1 cup crisp fried bacon bits (optional)
4 tablespoons soy sauce to serve

Equipment you'll need

sharp knife and chopping board

grater

measuring cups

wooden spoon

peeler

measuring spoons

wok

Mini shepherd's pies

Traditionally, shepherd's pie was made using leftovers from a Sunday roast lamb. But in case you don't have a cold roast hanging around the kitchen, you can make these mini versions with store-bought ground lamb or beef.

Ingredients you'll need

TOPPING
2½ lbs kg large potatoes, peeled and roughly chopped
1 cup milk
1 teaspoon butter
1 teaspoon salt
1⅓ cups grated cheddar cheese

FILLING
1 large onion, roughly chopped
2 tablespoons 2 teaspoons olive oil
1 lb ground lamb or beef
1 beef boullion cube
4 tablespoons tomato paste
½ teaspoon salt
2 pinches of black pepper
1 cup water

Equipment you'll need

sharp knife and chopping board
peeler
colander
potato masher
measuring spoons
large saucepan
oven mitts
mixing bowl
wooden spoon
food processor
medium frying pan
3 x 4⅓ in small ovenproof bowls
measuring cups
grater

* To make the topping, first **ask a grown-up** to help you prepare the potatoes and cook them in a large saucepan of boiling water until they are soft. It will probably take about 8–10 minutes. Drain the potatoes in a colander.

* Pour the milk into the same saucepan and **ask a grown-up** to help bring it to a simmer over a medium heat. Take the saucepan off the heat and carefully scoop the potatoes in. Leave them to sit for 2 minutes.

* Add the butter, salt, and ⅓ cup of grated cheese to the potatoes. Mash them thoroughly with a masher until there are no more lumps. It's a good idea to wear oven mitts to protect you from any hot steam.

* **Ask a grown-up** to help you preheat the oven to 350°F.

* To make the filling, **ask a grown-up** to help you put the onion into a food processor and blitz it to a paste. Once the grown-up has removed the blade from the processor, scrape the paste into a small bowl.

* Measure the oil into a frying pan and **ask a grown-up** to help you fry the onion paste over a medium heat. Add the ground meat and break it up with a wooden spoon as it cooks. This is important to make sure the meat is cooked all the way through and the sauce is not lumpy. Cook until browned all over.

* Crumble in the bullion cube then add the tomato paste, salt, pepper, and water. Stir everything together gently so it is evenly combined. Simmer for about 15 minutes or until all the water has evaporated, leaving a thick meaty sauce. **Ask a grown-up** to help you remove the frying pan from the heat and leave it to cool for a few minutes.

* Spoon the filling evenly between the 8 ovenproof bowls. Spread a large spoonful of mash over each pie then sprinkle with the rest of the grated cheese.

* **Ask a grown-up** to help you put the pies in the oven and bake for 20 minutes until the tops are golden brown. Remove from the oven and serve with a garden salad.

* *Makes 8 pies*

Potato croquettes

Croquettes are made from mashed potato and they are crunchy on the outside and lovely and soft in the middle. They can be made into small patties, balls, or little logs—whatever you feel like, really!

* **Ask a grown-up** to help you prepare the potatoes and cook them in a large saucepan of boiling water until they are soft. It will probably take about 8–10 minutes. Drain the potatoes in a colander and leave them to cool slightly.

* Return the potatoes to the saucepan and add the salt and pepper. Mash the potatoes thoroughly with a masher until there are no more lumps. It's a good idea to wear oven mitts to protect you from any hot steam.

* Stir in the grated cheese, chopped parsley, and the egg yolk and mix very well with a wooden spoon.

* Use a ¼-cup measure to scoop up some of the mixture, then use clean hands to form it into an oval egg shape. Place it on a cookie sheet, then continue until you have used up all the mixture—you should have about 12–14 patties in total.

* **Ask a grown-up** to help you set up 2 bowls on your kitchen counter. Put the beaten eggs in one bowl and the breadcrumbs in the other bowl.

* Dip the croquettes into the egg and then into the breadcrumbs, making sure they are coated all over. Place them back on the cookie sheet and place them in the fridge for 20–30 minutes to firm up.

* Dip the chilled croquettes into the egg and breadcrumbs again to form a thicker, crunchier coating and return them to the fridge for another 5–10 minutes.

* Measure the oil into the deep frying pan. **Ask a grown-up** to help you heat it over a medium heat. Carefully place 3–4 patties into the pan and cook them for 2 minutes. Use tongs to turn them over in the oil and cook them for another 2 minutes so they are golden brown and crunchy all over. Lift them out of the pan and onto paper towels to drain.

* Repeat with the rest of the croquettes until they are all cooked, then arrange them on a platter and serve them while they are piping hot.

* *Makes 12–14 croquettes*

Ingredients you'll need

2 lbs potatoes, peeled and roughly chopped
½ teaspoon salt
3 pinches of black pepper
1¾ cups grated parmesan cheese
3 large sprigs of parsley, finely chopped
1 egg yolk
3 eggs, beaten
2 cups homemade breadcrumbs
1 cup vegetable oil

Equipment you'll need

sharp knife and chopping board

peeler

large saucepan

colander

grater

potato masher

oven mitts

2 small bowls

wooden spoon

measuring cups

paper towels

cookie sheet

large deep frying pan

tongs

Soft in the middle

Crunchy on the outside

Croquettes are made from mashed potato.

Bite-sized BLTs

Make these sandwiches for your friends when they drop by after school. I guarantee they'll love them and they'll love you for making them!

Ingredients you'll need

1 teaspoon olive oil
8 bacon "eyes" (the round part of the bacon slice is called the "eye")
8 slices of square white bread, lightly toasted
5 tablespoons 1 teaspoon mayonnaise
½ cup grated cheddar cheese
4 lettuce leaves, cut in half (8 leaves in total)
1 large tomato, thinly sliced

Equipment you'll need

sharp knife and chopping board

grater   spatula

measuring spoons

frying pan

paper towels

measuring cups

large cookie sheet

toaster

toothpicks

tongs

* **Ask a grown-up** to help you preheat the oven to 350°F.

* Measure the oil into a frying pan and **ask a grown-up** to heat it over a medium heat. Fry the bacon until crisp, then carefully lift it onto paper towels to drain.

* Place 2 slices of toast on a chopping board and top each with ¾ tablespoon of mayonnaise. Spread it on evenly. Sprinkle a little grated cheese onto one piece of toast and top it with a piece of crispy bacon, a slice of tomato, and a lettuce leaf. Place the "lid" on top (mayo side down!). Repeat until all the sandwiches are made.

* **Ask a grown-up** to help you cut each sandwich into 4 little triangles. Stick a toothpick through each triangle and place them on a cookie sheet.

* **Ask a grown-up** to put the tray into the oven and heat the sandwiches for 5 minutes.

* To serve, use tongs to carefully arrange the sandwiches on a platter.

* *Makes 4 BLTs*

Sausage rolls

These sausage rolls are fantastic—everyone who tries them is hooked! Get a few of your friends to help you make a big batch for your next birthday party.

* **Ask a grown-up** to help you preheat the oven to 350°F. Grease the cookie sheets with the butter.

* **Ask a grown-up** to help you put the onion into a food processor and blitz it to a paste. Once the grown-up has removed the blade from the processor, scrape the paste into a mixing bowl.

* Add the grated carrot, cooked rice, breadcrumbs, and ground sausage to the bowl. Use scissors to snip the parsley and chives into the bowl then add the salt and pepper. Make sure your hands are very clean then use them to scrunch all the ingredients together with your fingers until they are evenly mixed.

* **Ask a grown-up** to help you cut each sheet of pastry in half. Lay a piece of the pastry out on a clean work surface. Use a ½-cup measure to scoop up a portion of the sausage mixture and place it on top of the pastry. Use your fingers to form it into a long sausage that goes along the center of the pastry; try to make it the same thickness all the way along. Roll the pastry over the sausage, then fold up the bottom of the pastry to meet it—it should overlap a little bit. Carefully turn the long sausage roll over so the seam is underneath. Repeat with the remaining pieces of pastry and the rest of the sausage mixture.

* **Ask a grown-up** to help you cut each long roll into 7 equal pieces.

* Place the sausage rolls on cookie sheets, leaving a little space between them. Brush the top of each sausage roll with a little beaten egg.

* **Ask a grown-up** to help you put the sheets in the oven and bake for 15 minutes or until the pastry is golden and flaky.

* When they are cooked, **ask a grown-up** to take them out of the oven. Arrange the sausage rolls on a platter and serve with tomato sauce if you like.

* *Makes around 70 sausage rolls*

Ingredients you'll need

1 tablespoon 1 teaspoon butter for greasing
1 large onion, roughly chopped
5 small carrots, peeled and grated
2 cups cooked, cooled brown rice
1 cup homemade breadcrumbs
1 lb ground sausage
3 sprigs of parsley
10 chives
2 teaspoons salt
3 pinches of black pepper
5 sheets of store-bought puff pastry
1 egg, beaten
tomato sauce to serve (optional)

Equipment you'll need

sharp knife and chopping board

food processor

large mixing bowl

peeler

measuring spoons

measuring cups

grater

large cookie sheets

scissors

tongs

pastry brush

Tasty tuna bake

This is a fantastic recipe to make whenever you have any leftover rice in the fridge. Most of us love tuna, and the golden cheese topping makes it extra tasty.

Ingredients you'll need

1 small red bell pepper, seeds and white membrane removed
1 medium onion, roughly chopped
2 tablespoons 2 teaspoons olive oil
1 tablespoon 1 teaspoon tomato paste
½ cup milk
1 tablespoon 1 teaspoon all-purpose flour
½ teaspoon salt
3 pinches of black pepper
1 x 15 oz can of tuna
1½ cups cooked white rice
1½ cups grated cheddar cheese

Equipment you'll need

sharp knife and chopping board

food processor

spatula

cake slice or egg flip

medium frying pan

oven mitts

measuring spoons

9 in baking dish

grater

measuring cups

wooden spoon

mixing bowl

* **Ask a grown-up** to help you preheat the oven to 350°F.

* **Ask a grown-up** to help you put the bell pepper and onion into a food processor and blitz it to a paste. You may need to scrape the sides down with a spatula to ensure all the big bits get properly chopped up. Once the grown-up has removed the blade from the processor, scrape the paste into a small bowl.

* Measure the oil into a frying pan and **ask a grown-up** to help you heat it over a medium heat. Carefully scrape the paste into the frying pan. It's best to wear oven mitts while you do this, in case it splatters. Add the tomato paste and fry for about 10 minutes, stirring every now and then.

* Add the milk, flour, salt, and pepper to the frying pan. Mix well and cook over low heat for a couple of minutes.

* **Ask a grown-up** to help you lift the pan off the heat. Add the tuna, breaking up the chunks carefully and mixing it in very well.

* Spread the cooked rice over the base of the baking dish. Spoon in the tuna mixture and spread it over the rice. Finally, top with the grated cheese.

* **Ask a grown-up** to put the tuna bake into the oven and cook for 14 minutes, or until the cheese is golden.

* **Ask a grown-up** to remove the baking dish from the oven and divide it into 4 big portions. It's best to wear oven mitts to protect you from any hot steam. Lift the squares onto a plate using a cake slice or egg flip and serve it immediately.

* *Makes 4 very hearty portions*

Chicken soup with tiny pasta

My mother used to make this soup with pastina, which is the Italian name for tiny pasta. You can use any shape you like.

* Put the pasta shapes into a medium saucepan. **Ask a grown-up** to help you boil a kettle then pour the water into the pan. Boil the pasta for 5 minutes, then drain in a colander.

* **Ask a grown-up** to pour the chicken stock into a large saucepan. Crumble in the boullion cube, add the salt, and stir well. Bring to a boil over a medium heat.

* **Ask a grown-up** to help you snip the scallion and chive into a bowl and mix with the shredded chicken.

* When the stock comes to a boil **ask a grown-up** to help you add the shredded chicken, scallions, chives, and cooked pasta shapes to the pan. Simmer gently for 2 minutes.

* **Ask a grown-up** to ladle the soup between 4 small bowls or mugs and serve it immediately.

* *Serves 4 small bowls of soup*

Ingredients you'll need

½ cup tiny pasta shapes
4¼ cups chicken stock
1 chicken boullion cube
½ teaspoon salt
1 scallion
1 chive
½ breast fillet from leftover roast or BBQ chicken, shredded

Equipment you'll need

measuring cups
saucepans
mixing bowl
measuring spoons
scissors
ladle
colander

Little egg and bacon breakfast pies

These make a great breakfast treat. If you want to speed things up, then it's a great idea to prepare the pastry shells ahead of time.

Ingredients you'll need

1 teaspoon butter for greasing
2 sheets of store-bought puff pastry
½ teaspoon olive oil
2 bacon "eyes" (the round part of the bacon slice is called the "eye"), cut into small cubes
½ small onion, roughly chopped
2 eggs
¼ cup milk
1 pinch of salt
2 pinches of black pepper
3 chives

Equipment you'll need

sharp knife and chopping board

food processor

2 x 4 in squares baking paper

ceramic pie weights or dried beans

ladle

measuring spoons

measuring cups

fork

muffin tray

frying pan

mixing bowls

scissors

---

* **Ask a grown-up** to help you preheat the oven to 350°F. Grease 6 holes of the muffin tray with the butter.

* Lay out the sheets of puff pastry on your work surface. Use a small bowl to cut out 6 pastry circles that will fit inside the muffin tray.

* Line the muffin holes with a pastry circle, pushing it in carefully but neatly. Prick the pastry a few times with a fork. Place a square of baking paper in each muffin hole and fill it with pie weights.

* **Ask a grown-up** to help you put the muffin tray on the bottom shelf of the oven and bake for 15 minutes. Take the tray out of the oven and carefully lift out the baking paper and pie weights. The pastry shells can be made to this stage ahead of time.

* Measure the oil into a frying pan and **ask a grown-up** to help you fry the bacon over a low–medium heat. Place the cooked bacon into a mixing bowl.

* **Ask a grown-up** to help you put the onion into a food processor and blitz it to a paste. Once the grown-up has removed the blade from the processor, scrape the paste into the mixing bowl with the bacon.

* Combine the eggs, milk, salt, and pepper in another mixing bowl and beat together well. Pour the mixture into the mixing bowl with the bacon and onion. Use scissors to snip in the chives and stir them in well.

* Use the ladle to divide the mixture evenly between the 6 pastry cases in the muffin tin. **Ask a grown-up** to help you put the tray in the oven and bake the pies for 20 minutes.

* Once a grown-up has taken the tray out of the oven, let them cool for a few minutes then carefully lift the pies out of the muffin holes and serve immediately.

* *Makes 6 pies*

Meatballs

These were something my mum used to make when I was little. You can serve them the Italian way in a tomato sauce with spaghetti, or you can serve them with mashed potatoes and salad—or even with mushy peas.

∗ If you're having a BBQ, this meatball mix also makes excellent burgers! Just take ¼-cup scoops of the mixture and shape them into round flat patties instead of meatballs.

∗ **Ask a grown-up** to help you put the onion into a food processor and blitz it to a paste. Once the grown-up has removed the blade from the processor, scrape the paste into a mixing bowl.

∗ Add the salt and pepper then use the scissors to snip the parsley leaves into the bowl. Add the grated parmesan, breadcrumbs, and the ground chicken (or beef) to the bowl. Make sure your hands are very clean then use them to scrunch all the ingredients together with your fingers until they are evenly mixed. Add the lemon juice and use your hands to mix it in well.

∗ Measure out 1 level tablespoon of the meatball mixture and use damp hands to roll it into a neat ball. Place it on a cookie sheet and continue until you have used up all the mixture.

∗ Measure half the oil into a frying pan and **ask a grown-up** to help you heat it over a medium heat. Carefully place some of the meatballs in the pan and fry for about 8 minutes until they are brown all over and cooked through. **Ask a grown-up** to help you with this and stand well back in case the oil splatters.

∗ Use the tongs to lift the cooked meatballs out of the pan and onto a paper towel to drain. It's a good idea to wear oven mitts while you do this in case the oil splatters.

∗ Repeat until all the meatballs are cooked.

∗ Arrange the meatballs on a platter and serve them right away.

∗ *Makes around 30 meatballs*

Ingredients you'll need

1 small onion, roughly chopped
½ teaspoon salt
3 pinches of black pepper
1 sprig of parsley
1½ cups grated parmesan cheese
1 cup homemade breadcrumbs
1 lb ground chicken or beef
juice of 1 small lemon
5 tablespoons 1 teaspoon olive oil for frying

Equipment you'll need

sharp knife and chopping board

food processor

large mixing bowl

scissors

measuring spoons

measuring cups

large cookie sheet

lemon juicer

large frying pan

oven mitts

paper towels

tongs

Crunchy chicken fingers

In this recipe the chicken fingers are oven-baked, not fried, which uses less oil and makes them healthier.

Ingredients you'll need

8 tablespoons olive oil

1 egg

6 tablespoons 2 teaspoons milk

¾ cup all-purpose flour

2 ⅓ cups homemade breadcrumbs

2 chicken breast fillets (approximately 1 lb), trimmed of fat and sinews and cut into 2⅓-in strips

Equipment you'll need

sharp knife and chopping board

whisk

measuring spoons

measuring cups

mixing bowls

tongs

2 large cookie sheets

* **Ask a grown-up** to help you preheat the oven to 320°F. Measure out 5 tablespoons of the olive oil and use it to grease 2 large cookie sheets.

* **Ask a grown-up** to help you set up 3 bowls on your kitchen counter. In one bowl, whisk together the egg with the milk. Put the flour into the second bowl and the breadcrumbs into the third bowl.

* Dip the chicken strips into the flour (about 5 pieces at a time) and roll them around so they are completely coated in the flour. Now dip them into the egg mixture so they are well coated. Lastly, roll the eggy strips around in the breadcrumbs. You need to press them down quite firmly to help the crumbs stick.

* Place the crumbed chicken fingers onto the greased oven trays so they are a little bit apart. Drizzle the remaining 3 tablespoons of oil over the top.

* **Ask a grown-up** to place the trays in the oven and cook for about 15 minutes, or until the strips are lightly golden. Remove the trays from the oven.

* Arrange the crunchy chicken fingers on a platter and serve immediately.

* *Makes 8 snack-sized servings*

28

Silly oven-baked chicken fingers

Honey and soy chicken kebabs

In this recipe, you need to soak your skewers in water before cooking as this stops the bamboo from burning.

* Thread the chicken cubes onto the prepared skewers. Try to put about the same number of cubes on each skewer.

* Mix the honey and soy sauce together in a baking dish. Place the skewers in the dish and turn them over so they are evenly coated with the marinade.

* **Ask a grown-up** to help you cover the baking dish with plastic wrap, then put it in the fridge and leave to marinate for at least 2 hours. If you leave it to marinate overnight the flavors will be even better. Turn the skewers over in the marinade every now and then so they soak up the flavors evenly.

* Measure the oil into a frying pan (or brush it onto a griddle) and **ask a grown-up** to help you heat it over a high heat. Reduce the heat to medium–low and cook the kebabs for about 3 minutes on each side. **Ask a grown-up** to help you with this and stand well back in case the oil splatters.

* Use tongs to arrange the kebabs on a serving platter and serve them with rice, if you desire.

* *Makes 10 small skewers*

Ingredients you'll need

2 chicken breast fillets (approximately 1 lb), cut into ¾-in cubes
⅓ cup honey
¼ cup soy sauce
2 tablespoons 2 teaspoons olive oil
2–3 cups cooked jasmine rice to serve (optional)
2 tomatoes, sliced to serve (optional)

Equipment you'll need

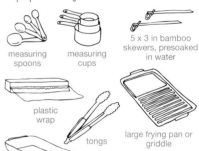

measuring spoons

measuring cups

5 x 3 in bamboo skewers, presoaked in water

plastic wrap

tongs

large frying pan or griddle

baking dish

Perfect potato gnocchi

For really light, smooth gnocchi, it's a good idea to use a mouli or potato ricer; you can buy them from specialty food stores.

Ingredients you'll need

1 lb potatoes, peeled and roughly chopped
4 tablespoons all-purpose flour for dusting the work surface
¼ teaspoon salt
1 cup all-purpose flour (use Tipo "00" flour, if possible)
3⅓ tablespoons butter
1½ cups grated parmesan

Equipment you'll need

sharp knife and chopping board
large saucepan with lid
peeler
slotted spoon
colander
measuring spoons
grater
ladle
small saucepan
mouli or potato ricer
measuring cups
tea towel

* **Ask a grown-up** to help you prepare the potatoes and bring a large saucepan of water to a boil. When the water is boiling, carefully add the potatoes. Stand well back, in case there is any splashing.

* Cook the potatoes until they are soft. It will probably take about 8–10 minutes. Drain the potatoes in a colander and leave them to cool slightly.

* Sprinkle the 4 tablespoons of flour onto the work surface. **Ask a grown-up** to help you put the potatoes into a mouli or potato ricer and push them directly onto the floured work surface.

* Sprinkle the salt and ⅓ cup of flour over the potato. Make sure your hands are very clean then mix it in quickly. Add the rest of the flour in two more batches, mixing each in quickly and lightly; you don't want to overwork the gnocchi dough.

* Divide the dough into thirds and roll each into a long rope, about ¾ in thick. Cut each rope into ¾ in pieces.

* **Ask a grown-up** to help you bring another large saucepan of water to a boil. Carefully drop in half the gnocchi. After a few minutes they will start to rise to the surface. As they do, use a slotted spoon to lift them out and place them on a clean tea towel to drain. Repeat until all the gnocchi are cooked.

* Put the butter into a small saucepan and **ask a grown-up** to help you melt it over a medium heat until it turns a light golden brown. As soon as it does, take the pan off the heat to stop the butter from burning.

* Divide the gnocchi among 4 shallow serving bowls and ladle on the hot butter. Top each portion with parmesan cheese and serve right away.

* *Makes 4 servings of gnocchi*

Yummy mini burgers

These burgers are really easy to make and are great to serve for dinner.

* **Ask a grown-up** to help you put the onion into a food processor and blitz it to a paste. Once the grown-up has removed the blade from the processor, scrape the paste into a mixing bowl.

* Add the grated apple, ground meat, and beaten egg to the bowl. Use scissors to snip in the chives then add the salt and pepper. Use a wooden spoon to mix everything together thoroughly.

* Use a ¼-cup measure to scoop up some of the mixture, then use clean hands to form it into a burger, about ⅓ in thick. Place it on a cookie sheet, then continue until you have used up all the mixture—you should have about 12 burgers in total.

* Measure the oil into the frying pan and **ask a grown-up** to help you heat it over a medium–low heat. Carefully add the burgers, about 6 at a time, and fry them for 5 minutes on each side, or until cooked through. It's best to wear oven mitts when you flip the burgers over, in case the oil splatters.

* Carefully lift the burgers out of the pan and onto paper towels to drain. Repeat with the rest of the burgers until they are all cooked.

* While the burgers are frying, split the mini buns in half and toast the insides underneath the broiler.

* To serve, place a burger onto the bottom half of each mini bun. Top with a slice of tomato and a little shredded lettuce. If you like, spoon on a little apple sauce or catsup. Place the "lid" on top and eat right away.

* *Makes 12 mini burgers*

Ingredients you'll need

1 medium onion, finely chopped
2 large apples, peeled and grated
1 lb ground chicken, beef, or pork
1 egg, beaten
12 chives
1 teaspoon salt
2 pinches of black pepper
⅓ cup vegetable oil for frying
12 mini buns
2 medium-sized tomatoes, each cored and cut into 6 slices
12 iceberg lettuce leaf pieces
12 teaspoons store-bought apple sauce or catsup (optional)

Equipment you'll need

sharp knife and chopping board

mixing bowl

food processor

scissors

measuring spoons

measuring cups

wooden spoon

egg flip

peeler

oven mitts

large frying pan

grater

Juicy tomato salad

In true Italian style, this dish is best eaten with your hands and crusty bread. It will be a bit messy but that's part of the fun!

Ingredients you'll need

3 medium ripe tomatoes, cored and cut into eighths
½ small onion, very finely sliced
4 tablespoons olive oil
½ teaspoon salt
½ loaf casalinga bread (or any crusty sourdough)

Equipment you'll need

sharp knife and chopping board

mixing bowl

measuring spoons

serrated knife

* In a large mixing bowl, combine the tomatoes and onion. Pour on the oil and add the salt. Use the salad tongs to mix everything together very well. Make sure there are no big clumps of onion left in the salad. The more you stir, the more juice your tomatoes will release. Leave the salad to sit for about 10 minutes before serving.

* Use a serrated bread knife to cut the bread into about ⅓ in slices.

* To serve, spoon some tomato salad onto each plate and drizzle with some of the tomatoey juices. Serve with slices of bread for dipping and mopping.

* *Makes 4 small servings*

Variations

* For a change, you can add a scattering of yellow pear tomatoes or cherry tomatoes (about 6) to this dish.

* Serve a little bowl of shaved parmesan with this salad so that everyone can sprinkle a little cheese onto their portion. But only do it at the last minute or the cheese will get soggy.

Tacos

Mexican is a great cuisine to try out early on in your cooking adventures at home as you'll be able to do a lot of the meal preparation all by yourself.

* **Ask a grown-up** to help you preheat the oven to 350°F. Lay the taco shells on a cookie sheet.

* Measure the oil into a frying pan. **Ask a grown-up** to help you heat the frying pan over medium–low heat. Add the ground beef and break it up with a wooden spoon as it cooks. This is important to make sure the meat is cooked all the way through and the sauce is not lumpy. Cook until browned all over.

* Add the spice mix and water. Reduce the heat to low, then cover the frying pan and simmer for about 15 minutes or until all the water has evaporated, leaving a thick meaty sauce.

* **Ask a grown-up** to help you heat the taco shells in the oven for 3 minutes.

* Divide the meat sauce evenly between the taco shells. Top with shredded lettuce, diced tomato, salsa, and grated cheese.

* Serve the tacos immediately, or **ask a grown-up** to help you put the tacos back in the oven for another 5 minutes so the cheese starts to melt.

* *Makes 10 tacos*

Ingredients you'll need

10 hard, flat-bottomed taco shells

2 tablespoons 2 teaspoons olive oil

1 lb ground beef

1 x 1¼ oz packet of taco spice mix (some health-food shops sell excellent, healthy pre-made spice mixes)

¾ cup water

¼ iceberg lettuce, shredded

3 medium tomatoes, cored and chopped into small cubes

10 teaspoons mild salsa

1 cup grated cheddar cheese

Equipment you'll need

sharp knife and chopping board

grater

large cookie sheet

measuring spoons

frying pan with a lid

measuring cups

wooden spoon

The ticklish taco twins . . .

Tuna patties

You can show off your cooking skills and cook these patties at your next family BBQ.

Ingredients you'll need

1 lb large floury potatoes, peeled and chopped
2 x 6½ oz cans of tuna in oil, drained
4 chives
2 sprigs of parsley
1 scallion
1 large onion, roughly chopped
½ teaspoon salt
3 pinches of black pepper
2 eggs
1 cup homemade breadcrumbs
¼ cup olive oil for frying

Equipment you'll need

sharp knife and chopping board

large saucepan

potato masher

large mixing bowl

colander

grater

oven mitts

measuring spoons

food processor

measuring cups

scissors

large cookie sheet

large frying pan

paper towel

tongs

* **Ask a grown-up** to help you prepare the potatoes and cook them in a large saucepan of boiling water until they are soft. It will probably take about 8–10 minutes. Drain them in a colander then place them into a large mixing bowl to cool down a bit.

* Mash the potatoes with a masher until there are no more lumps. It's a good idea to wear oven mitts to protect you from any hot steam.

* Add the tuna to the potato and mash it in well so there are no more chunks. Using scissors, carefully snip the chives, parsley, and scallion into the bowl with the tuna mash.

* **Ask a grown-up** to help you put the onion into a food processor and blitz it to a paste. Once the grown-up has removed the blade from the processor, scrape the paste into the mixing bowl with the tuna mash. Add the salt and pepper and crack in 1 egg, then stir everything together so it is very well combined.

* Use a ¼-cup measure to scoop up some of the mixture, then use clean hands to form it into a round, flat patty. Place it on a cookie sheet, then continue until you have used up all the mixture—you should have about 14 patties in total. Leave space between the patties so they don't stick together. Place them in the fridge for 15–20 minutes to firm up.

* **Ask a grown-up** to help you set up 2 bowls on your kitchen bench. Whisk the second egg in one bowl and put the breadcrumbs into the other bowl.

* Dip the chilled patties into the egg and then into the breadcrumbs, making sure they are coated all over.

* Measure the oil into the frying pan. **Ask a grown-up** to help you heat it over a low–medium heat. Carefully place 3–4 patties into the pan and cook them for 3–4 minutes. Use tongs to turn them over and cook them for another 3–4 minutes. They should be golden brown and crunchy all over. **Ask a grown-up** to help you lift them out of the pan and onto paper towels to drain.

* Repeat with the rest of the patties until they are all cooked, then serve them with a big salad.

* *Makes around 14 patties*

Pasta bake

As a friend of mine once said, "Cheese improves everything!" Although this isn't the healthiest rule to follow, I think it is true with this dish. Make the sauce while the pasta is cooking, and both should be ready at the same time.

* **Ask a grown-up** to help you fill a large saucepan two-thirds full with cold water, then bring it to a boil. Add the pasta and stir it gently. Boil for about 8 minutes (or check the instructions on the packet), until it is just "al dente"*. Drain the pasta in a colander.

* **Ask a grown-up** to help you preheat the oven to 350°F.

* Measure the oil into the dried-out saucepan and **ask a grown-up** to help you heat it over a low heat. Add the garlic to the pan and fry until lightly golden, stirring with a wooden spoon. Turn the heat off and leave it to cool for 3 minutes.

* **Ask a grown-up** to help you pour the passata into the pan. It's best to wear oven mitts, although if you have cooled the oil enough it shouldn't splatter. Now add the sugar, baking soda, salt, pepper, and water to the pan. Add the parsley leaves and stir the sauce gently. Cook over a medium–low heat for 20 minutes, stirring it every now and then.

* **Ask a grown-up** to help you pour the drained pasta into the sauce, then add the flaked tuna. Stir so everything is mixed together well. Now **ask a grown-up** to help you carefully pour the pasta mix into a baking dish. Sprinkle the cheese over the top and cook in the oven for 20 minutes or until the cheese is golden.

* **Ask a grown-up** to remove the pasta bake from the oven and to help you cut it into square portions. Lift the portions onto a plate using a cake slice or egg flip and serve it with a fresh garden salad and a little dish of tomato sauce or tomato chutney.

* *Makes 6 servings*

* "Al dente" means "tender to the bite" in Italian. "Al dente" pasta feels soft when you bite it but is still firm and holds its shape.

Ingredients you'll need

8¾ oz penne pasta

1 tablespoon 1 teaspoon olive oil

2 garlic cloves garlic, crushed

1¾ cups passata (tomato purée that you can buy from supermarkets)

1 teaspoon sugar

½ teaspoon baking soda

1 teaspoon salt

2 pinches of pepper

⅓ cup 1½ tablespoons water

2 sprigs of parsley

1 x 6½ oz can of tuna in oil, drained and separated into small chunks

3 cups grated cheddar cheese

Equipment you'll need

oven mitts

egg flip

large saucepan

wooden spoon

colander

baking dish (approximately 8 in × 8 in × 2in)

grater

garlic press

measuring jug, measuring cups, and measuring spoons

Cinnamon apple fritters

I recommend using Granny Smith apples in this recipe, but they will still turn out well if you use a different variety.

Ingredients you'll need
½ cup all-purpose flour
1 pinch of salt
1 egg, separated
⅓ cup milk
2 Granny Smith apples
¼ cup vegetable oil for frying
2 tablespoons 2 teaspoons raw sugar
for sprinkling
1 teaspoon ground cinnamon
for sprinkling

Equipment you'll need

sharp knife and chopping board
sifter
whisk
measuring cups
mixing bowls
electric mixer
measuring spoons
peeler
frying pan
paper towels
apple corer
tongs
large metal kitchen spoon

* Sift the flour and salt into a mixing bowl. Add the egg yolk, then pour in the milk. Whisk together to form a smooth batter. Try to make sure there are no lumpy bits.

* Pour the egg white into the bowl of an electric mixer and beat until it forms a thick white foam. It should be thick enough to form soft floppy peaks if you lift the beater out.

* **Ask a grown-up** to help you pour the egg white into the batter. Use a large kitchen spoon to stir them together, working from the middle of the bowl. Instead of stirring round and round, try to cut downwards through the mixture and then turn it over (this is called "folding"). The batter should be smooth, thick, and shiny.

* **Ask a grown-up** to help you peel and core the apples (this can be tricky, but there are also special machines that do both tasks at the same time). Slice the apples into about ¼ in rings—you should be able to get about 8 rings from each apple.

* Dip 3 apple rings into the batter and use tongs to turn them so they are coated all over.

* **Ask a grown-up** to heat the oil in a frying pan over a low–medium heat. When it is just hot, place the 3 apple rings in the oil. **Ask a grown-up** to do this for you and stand well back in case the oil splatters. Fry the fritters for 2 minutes on each side until the apple is soft and the fritters are golden.

* **Ask a grown-up** to help you lift the fritters out of the pan and onto paper towels to drain, then lift them onto a warm serving plate. Repeat with the remaining apple rings.

* Mix the sugar with the cinnamon in a small bowl. Sprinkle onto the hot fritters and serve them right away.

* *Makes around 16 fritters*

Special occasion trifle

This trifle looks very Christmassy with its red, white, and green topping. It is best to eat this dessert the day it's made, otherwise the bananas discolor and it doesn't look as impressive.

* To make the custard, combine the milk, cream, and vanilla in a saucepan. **Ask a grown-up** to help you heat it over a medium heat until it comes to a simmer. (The milk will become frothy and you will start to see bubbles forming.) Turn off the heat.

* Place the egg yolks and sugar in a large mixing bowl and whisk them together until light and foamy. **Ask a grown-up** to pour the hot milk and cream into the bowl very, very slowly while you keep whisking. It is a good idea for you to wear oven mitts while whisking in case the hot liquid splashes. Keep whisking while all the milk is being added so that the eggs don't curdle.

* **Ask a grown-up** to help you pour the mixture back into the saucepan over a low heat. Cook it for 10–15 minutes, stirring all the time with a wooden spoon, but be sure not to let it boil. If you get tired with all the stirring, **ask a grown-up** to help. Eventually it will start to thicken (and it will thicken more as it cools down). To test if it is done, **ask a grown-up** to dip a spoon into the custard. It should be thick enough to coat the back of the spoon and if you run your finger through it it should leave a clear line that holds its shape. When the custard is ready, **ask a grown-up** to help you pour it into a bowl. When it has cooled a little bit put it into the fridge to chill completely. If you don't want a skin to form on top of the custard, place a piece of plastic wrap directly on the surface.

* When you are ready to put the trifle together, **ask a grown-up** to help you cut the Swiss roll into about ½ in slices. Lay half in the bottom of a large trifle bowl and top with a layer of raspberries and banana slices. Spoon in half the custard to cover the sponge and the fruit. Repeat with another layer of cake slices, fruit, and custard.

* To make the topping, put the cream and vanilla into the bowl of an electric mixer. Beat it until it thickens enough to form soft, floppy peaks when you lift out the beater. Spoon the whipped cream onto the top of the trifle and use a spatula to smooth it out evenly. Cover the trifle with plastic wrap and chill it for 1–2 hours.

* While the trifle is chilling, **ask a grown-up** to help you lightly roast the slivered almonds in a dry frying pan.

* When ready to serve, sprinkle the nuts all over the top of the trifle, then decorate it with the reserved raspberries.

* *Makes 8 servings of trifle*

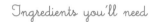

Ingredients you'll need

CUSTARD
1¾ cups milk
2½ cups cream
2 tablespoons 2 teaspoons vanilla-bean paste
10 egg yolks
½ cup granulated sugar

CAKE/FRUIT LAYER
1 packet of store-bought Swiss roll
1 carton of raspberries (reserve 10 for decoration)
2 large bananas, sliced

TOPPING
1¼ cups cream
1 tablespoon 1 teaspoon vanilla-bean paste
¼ cup slivered almonds
¼ cup pistachio slivers

Equipment you'll need

sharp knife and chopping board

measuring jug, measuring cups, and measuring spoons

oven mitts

saucepan

plastic wrap

electric mixer

spatula

whisk

frying pan

mixing bowl

wooden spoon

Large trifle bowl (see-through bowl is preferable)

Shortcake

My top tip for making the lightest shortcakes is to use a very fine flour, like Italian Tipo "00," which you can buy at good supermarkets and food stores. I make baby-sized shortcakes; it takes a bit more time, but they are perfect for a party!

Ingredients you'll need

1 teaspoon butter for greasing
3 cups self-rising flour (preferably Tipo "00"), plus extra for dusting
½ teaspoon salt
¾ cup light cream
1 cup lemonade
whipped cream to serve
raspberry or strawberry jam to serve

Equipment you'll need

large cookie sheet

measuring jug, measuring cups, and measuring spoons

rolling pin

mixing bowl

sifter

wire rack

oven mitts

round cookie cutter

tongs

* **Ask a grown-up** to help you preheat the oven to 320°F and grease a large cookie sheet.

* Sift the flour into a large mixing bowl. Add the salt, cream, and lemonade and use clean hands to mix everything together, but just until it is combined and smooth. It is important not to overwork shortcakes.

* Dump the shortcake dough out of the bowl onto a work surface lightly dusted with flour. Pat it into a round ball then roll it gently with a rolling pin until it is about ⅓ in thick. Dip the cookie cutter in flour then cut out rounds from the dough. Gather up all the leftover bits into a ball, then roll it out again and cut out more rounds.

* Place the shortcake onto the cookie sheet, arranging them about ⅓ in apart. **Ask a grown-up** to help you put the sheet into the oven and bake for 10–12 minutes until they are risen and golden. If you lift one up and tap the bottom, it should sound hollow. **Ask a grown-up** to help you with this and make sure you wear an oven mitt.

* **Ask a grown-up** to help you take the sheet out of the oven and lift the shortcakes onto a wire rack to cool. Use tongs or an egg flip to do this.

* When the shortcakes have cooled a little bit, serve them with whipped cream and jam.

* *Makes around 56 baby-sized shortcakes*

Baby shortcakes—perfect for a party!

Sticky rosewater dumplings

These amazing sticky dumplings come from India. If you have roses in your garden, pick a few petals to scatter over as decoration.

Ingredients you'll need

SYRUP
6 ⅓ cups litres water
2 cups raw sugar
2 teaspoons ground cardamom
2 tablespoons 2 teaspoons rosewater

DUMPLINGS
2 cups all-purpose flour
2 teaspoons baking powder
1½ cups cream
2 tablespoons 2 teaspoons milk
2 teaspoons flour for dusting
5¼ cups vegetable oil for frying
whipped cream to serve (optional)

Equipment you'll need

saucepans

measuring spoons

measuring cups

measuring jug

mixing bowl

oven mitts

large cookie sheet

wooden spoon

tongs

slotted spoon

* To make the syrup, combine the water and sugar in a saucepan and **ask a grown-up** to help you heat it over a low–medium heat. Stir gently until the sugar has dissolved. It is a good idea to wear oven mitts while you do this to protect your hands from any hot splashes. Once the sugar has dissolved, bring the syrup to a boil, then lower the heat and let it simmer very gently with the lid off for an hour. It will reduce to form a thick syrup. **Ask a grown-up** to help you remove the pan from the heat. Stir in the cardamom and rosewater and leave it to cool.

* To make the dumplings, sift the flour and baking powder into a mixing bowl. Pour the cream and milk into a jug and pour it into the flour a little at a time. You might like to **ask a grown-up** to do the pouring while you stir it in with a wooden spoon. You should end up with a dough that is quite wet and sticky.

* Pour the dough out onto a work surface lightly dusted with flour. Dip your hands into a little flour as well, which will stop the dough sticking to them, and shape the dough into a rough ball. Take a ¾ tablespoon of the dough and roll it between your palms to make a smooth ball. Place the dumpling on a cookie sheet and repeat until you have used up all the dough.

* **Ask a grown-up** to help you heat the vegetable oil in a deep saucepan over a low heat. When bubbles just start to appear, fry the dumplings, a few at a time, turning them around in the oil so they are golden all over (make sure you stand well back in case the oil splatters). Use a slotted spoon to lift the dumplings out of the oil. Hold them over the pan until most of the oil has drained off then put them straight into the saucepan of sugar syrup. Repeat with the rest of the dumplings.

* Place dumplings in the large serving bowl. Drizzle syrup over them. Serve them with whipped cream if you like.

* *Makes around 52 dumplings*

Anzac cookies

Anzac cookies were named in honor of the Australian and New Zealand troops during the First World War. No eggs were used in the cookies so they didn't spoil on the long journey to the battle front.

* **Ask a grown-up** to help you preheat the oven to 320°F and grease several cookie sheets with the butter.

* Combine the oats, flour, coconut, and sugar in a large mixing bowl.

* Place the butter and light corn syrup in a saucepan and **ask a grown-up** to help you melt them over a medium heat. Stir so they are well mixed, then turn off the heat and let it cool a little.

* **Ask a grown-up** to help you add the baking soda to the boiling water in a little bowl, then pour it into the melted butter and syrup. It is best to wear oven mitts while you do this as the baking soda will foam up. Pour into the dry ingredients and stir in well with a wooden spoon.

* Place teaspoons of the cookie mixture onto the greased cookie sheets leaving about 2 in of space between them so they can spread out while cooking. Use your fingers to flatten them a little bit.

* **Ask a grown-up** to help you put the cookies in the oven and bake for 10 minutes, or until they are golden. Take the sheet out of the oven and use an egg flip to lift the cookies onto a wire rack to cool. They will firm up as they cool down.

* *Makes around 28* cookies

Ingredients you'll need

1 teaspoon butter for greasing
1 cup rolled oats
½ cup flour
½ cup flaked coconut
½ cup brown sugar
4¾ tablespoons butter
2 tablespoons 2 teaspoons light corn syrup
1 teaspoon baking soda
1 tablespoon 1 teaspoon boiling water

Equipment you'll need

measuring spoons

measuring cups

mixing bowls

saucepan

oven mitts

egg flip

wooden spoon

cookie sheets

wire rack

Ginger nut Christmas log

This dessert should be kept in the fridge for at least 2–6 hours before you want to serve it, so that it becomes soft and squishy.

Ingredients you'll need

1¼ cups cream
2 teaspoons vanilla-bean paste
8¾ oz packet of ginger nut cookies
2 tablespoons confectioners sugar
2 candy canes (optional) for decoration

Equipment you'll need

electric mixer

mini spatula

measuring spoons

confectioners sugar shaker

* Put the cream and vanilla into the bowl of an electric mixer. Beat it until it thickens enough to form stiff peaks when you lift out the beater.

* With a mini spatula, spread 1 tablespoon of cream over the surface of each ginger nut cookie until you have used up the whole packet.

* Sandwich the cookies together in little groups of 5. Carefully lay them on their side on a long serving platter to form a thin log, about 1 foot long. Use the mini spatula to spread the rest of the cream all over the log; don't forget the ends.

* Use the side of the spatula to carefully draw long wobbly stripes from one end of the log to the other to resemble the bark of a tree.

* **Ask a grown-up** to help you put the log into the fridge overnight—or for at least 2 hours. The ginger nut cookies will soften as the cream soaks in.

* Just before serving, dust the log all over with confectioners sugar. If you want to make it look really Christmassy, decorate it with candy canes. I like to stand one candy cane upright in the log and crush the other one finely and sprinkle it over the surface. Cut the log into slices on the diagonal instead of straight across.

* *Makes 8 slices*

Mini chocolate soufflés

Many kids find dark chocolate a little bitter, and like the sweetness of milk chocolate. So if you're making these soufflés for your friends, try using half dark and half milk chocolate instead.

* **Ask a grown-up** to help you preheat the oven to 390°F.
* Measure out 1⅓ tablespoons of the butter, place it in a saucepan, and **ask a grown-up** to help you melt it over a medium heat. Leave it to cool a little.
* Use a pastry brush to coat the insides of the soufflé dishes with melted butter. Make sure you brush in an upwards direction, as it helps the soufflé to rise upwards in the oven. Measure out 2 tablespoons 2 teaspoons of the granulated sugar and sprinkle a little inside each soufflé dish. Carefully roll the dishes along the work surface so that the sugar sticks to the butter and forms an even coating. Place the dishes on a cookie sheet.
* **Ask a grown-up** to help you put the saucepan back on a medium heat and melt the rest of the butter. Add the flour and whisk it in briskly until the mixture is smooth and starts to bubble.
* Add the milk, a little at a time. Whisk all the time so that the milk mixes in smoothly and there are no lumpy bits. Let it simmer for 1 minute then take it off the heat.
* Add the chopped chocolate and the rest of the granulated sugar to the hot mixture and stir until the chocolate has all melted. Add the egg yolks and mix them in until very smooth. **Ask a grown-up** to help you scrape all the mixture into a large mixing bowl and leave it to cool down a bit more.
* Put the egg whites into the bowl of an electric mixer and beat until they form a thick white foam with little peaks when you lift the beater out.
* **Ask a grown-up** to help you pour half of the egg whites onto the chocolate mixture. Use a large kitchen spoon to stir them together, working from the middle of the bowl. Instead of stirring round and round, try to cut downwards through the mixture and then turn it over (this is called "folding"). When nearly mixed in, add the rest of the egg whites and fold them in too. The soufflé mixture should be light and frothy and not streaky.
* Divide the soufflé mixture between the dishes then **ask a grown-up** to help you put them in the oven. Cook for 15 minutes without opening the oven door. When the soufflés are ready they should feel a bit springy and bouncy when you touch them. Slide a skewer into the center to make sure they are not runny underneath.
* **Ask a grown-up** to take the soufflés out of the oven and dust them with confectioners sugar. Take them to the table immediately and serve them with a dollop of whipped cream of you like.
* *Makes 6 mini soufflés*

Ingredients you'll need

4¾ tablespoons softened butter
6 tablespoons 2 teaspoons granulated sugar
2 tablespoons 2 teaspoons all-purpose flour
1 cup milk
2⅓ oz milk chocolate, roughly chopped
2⅓ oz dark chocolate, roughly chopped
4 eggs, separated
confectioners sugar to dust
whipped cream to serve (optional)

Equipment you'll need

sharp knife and chopping board

saucepan

pastry brush

wooden spoon

6 × 5½ oz soufflé dishes

cookie sheet

whisk

mixing bowl

electric mixer

confectioners sugar shaker

measuring cups

measuring spoons

large metal kitchen spoon

metal skewer

How high is your soufflé?

Shortbreads

At Christmas time you can turn these into star decorations for your tree. Just use the end of a drinking straw to punch a small hole through a point of each star before you cook them, then thread a ribbon through the hole.

* **Ask a grown-up** to help you preheat the oven to 360°F and grease a cookie sheet with the butter.

* Sift the flour into a mixing bowl and add the granulated sugar.

* Put the butter in a saucepan and **ask a grown-up** to help you melt it over a low heat. Turn off the heat and let it cool a little.

* **Ask a grown-up** to help you tip the butter onto the dry ingredients. Add the vanilla and stir with a wooden spoon until it comes together to form a rough ball. Place the dough onto a work surface lightly dusted with flour. Use clean hands to pat it into a round ball then roll it gently with a rolling pin until it is about 1/3 in thick.

* Dip the cookie cutter in flour then cut out cookies from the dough. Gather up all the leftover bits into a ball, then roll it out again and cut out more cookies.

* Place the cookies on the cookie sheet, arranging them about 1/3 in apart. If you are going to use the shortbreads as Christmas tree decorations then poke the holes in them now.

* **Ask a grown-up** to help you put the sheet into the oven and bake for 15 minutes. They will still be pale and soft when they come out of the oven, but will harden as they cool. Leave them on the sheet for 5 minutes without moving them, then use an egg flip to lift them onto a wire rack.

* *Makes around 30 shortbreads*

Ingredients you'll need

1 teaspoon butter for greasing
1 cup all-purpose flour, plus extra for dusting
1/3 cup granulated sugar
7½ tablespoons butter
½ teaspoon vanilla-bean paste

Equipment you'll need

measuring spoons
measuring cups
sifter
rolling pin
cookie sheet
mixing bowl
saucepan
cookie cutters
wooden spoon
drinking straws
egg flip
wire rack

Gingerbread snowflakes

I like to make snowflake-shaped gingerbread cookies, but of course you can make them any shape that you like.

Ingredients you'll need

1 tablespoon 1 teaspoon butter for greasing
2 ¼ cups all-purpose flour
½ tablespoon baking soda
¼ teaspoon salt
1 teaspoon ground ginger
¼ teaspoon ground cinnamon
¼ teaspoon ground nutmeg
¼ teaspoon ground cardamom
1 teaspoon grated orange zest plus
2 tablespoons 2 teaspoons orange juice
1 teaspoon grated lemon zest plus
2 tablespoons 2 teaspoons lemon juice
5 tablespoons butter
½ cup light corn syrup
2 tablespoons 2 teaspoons brown sugar
1 teaspoon all-purpose flour for dusting
confectioners sugar for dusting

Equipment you'll need

mixing bowl

zester

large cookie sheets

confectioners sugar shaker

rolling pin

measuring spoons

measuring cups

saucepan

plastic wrap

wire rack

lemon juicer

wooden spoon

egg flip

large cookie sheets

cookie cutters

sifter

* **Ask a grown-up** to help you preheat the oven to 320°F and grease several cookie sheets with the butter.

* Sift the flour and baking soda into a large mixing bowl and add the salt, spices, and citrus zests.

* Measure the orange and lemon juice into a saucepan. Add the butter, light corn syrup and brown sugar and **ask a grown-up** to help you heat it over a low heat. Stir everything gently until the butter has melted and the syrup and sugar have dissolved. Don't allow the mixture to become too hot. Turn off the heat and leave to cool for 5 minutes.

* **Ask a grown-up** to help you pour the melted mixture into the dry ingredients. Mix together very well with a wooden spoon. The mixture will be quite firm, so you may need to **ask a grown-up** to help you with this. As soon as it comes together to form a ball scoop it out onto a work surface dusted with flour.

* Use clean hands to shape it into a smooth round, then wrap it in a piece of plastic wrap. Put it in the fridge for 20 minutes to chill and firm up.

* Unwrap the dough and **ask a grown-up** to help you cut it into quarters. With clean hands, shape each into a round ball, then roll them gently with a rolling pin until they are about ⅓ in thick. Cut out cookies from the dough using cutters, then lift them carefully onto the prepared cookie sheets, arranging them about 2 in apart so they can spread out while cooking. Gather up all the leftover bits of dough into a ball, then roll it out again and cut out more cookies.

* **Ask a grown-up** to help you put the sheets into the oven and bake for 6–7 minutes until golden.

* **Ask a grown-up** to help you take the sheets out of the oven. The cookies will still be soft when they come out, but will harden as they cool. Leave them on the tray for 5 minutes without moving them, then use an egg flip to lift them onto a wire rack.

* When the gingerbread cookies are completely cold, dust them with confectioners sugar (or frost them, if you prefer).

* *Makes 22 large snowflake cookies*

Apple tea cake

This is a simple recipe as you don't have to cook the apples first. They cook with the cake, and the cinnamon and sugar create a lovely topping.

* **Ask a grown-up** to help you preheat the oven to 360°F and grease a baking pan with the butter.

* Sift the flour and baking powder salt into a large mixing bowl and add the salt and 5 tablespoons of the sugar. Stir everything around so it is mixed together well.

* Add the butter to the bowl and use clean fingers to rub it into the dry ingredients until it all looks like fine breadcrumbs.

* Place the egg and milk into another mixing bowl and whisk them together well. Pour into the dry ingredients and whisk until the mixture becomes a smooth batter.

* **Ask a grown-up** to help you pour the batter into the baking pan and arrange the pieces of apple on top. Press them in gently so they sink in just a little bit.

* Mix the remaining 3 tablespoons of sugar with the cinnamon and sprinkle it evenly over the top of the cake.

* **Ask a grown-up** to help you put the cake in the oven and bake for 30–40 minutes or until cooked through. The cake is done when a skewer inserted into the middle comes out cleanly. Take the cake out of the oven and let it cool a few minutes.

* **Ask a grown-up** to help you remove the cake from the tin. Use a spatula to loosen it a little bit around the edges, then place a plate on top of the tin and quickly flip everything upside down so the cake falls out of the tin onto the plate. Now turn the cake back the right way up onto a wire cake rack.

* Serve the cake while it is still warm, with whipped cream if you like.

* *Serves 8 slices of cake*

Ingredients you'll need

1 teaspoon butter for greasing
1½ cups all-purpose flour
1½ teaspoons baking powder
½ teaspoon salt
8 tablespoons sugar
¼ cup slightly softened butter
1 egg
¾ cup milk
2 medium apples, peeled, cored, and cut into eighths
½ teaspoon ground cinnamon
whipped cream to serve (optional)

Equipment you'll need

measuring spoons

measuring cups

sharp knife and chopping board

wooden spoon

sifter

peeler

mixing bowls

whisk

spatula

metal skewer

square baking pan

wire rack

Tutti frutti salad

This great summery salad looks spectacular with its vibrant colors, and it tastes so fresh and healthy. You'll feel great after eating this!

Ingredients you'll need

1 carton of ripe strawberries
2 just-ripe mangoes
2 slices of watermelon
1 large orange
1 small lemon
2 tablespoons 2 teaspoons honey
1 carton of raspberries
12 mint leaves

Equipment you'll need

sharp knife and chopping board

peeler

lemon juicer

measuring spoons

teaspoon

large glass serving bowl

container with a tight-fitting lid (a screw-top jar is perfect)

* **Ask a grown-up** to help you prepare all the fruit. First slice the green leaves and tops off the strawberries and cut them in half.

* Use a sharp knife to cut the "cheeks" (the wide sides) off the mangoes. Score mango flesh (the soft inside) with the knife in a crisscross pattern to make squares. Turn the mango cheeks inside-out and use a teaspoon to scoop out all the little squares.

* Cut the rind off the watermelon slices, then use your fingers to pick out all the seeds and discard them. Chop the watermelon into ⅓ in cubes.

* Cut the orange and lemon in half and juice them. Pour the juice into a container and add the honey and vanilla. Put the lid on and give it a good shake to mix everything together.

* Gently combine all the fruit in a large glass serving bowl. Pour on the sweet juices and use salad servers to toss everything together gently. Top with mint leaves.

* *Makes 6 servings*

Christmassy punch

This is a lovely refreshing punch to serve on Christmas day—even the colors go with the Christmas theme!

* **Ask a grown-up** to help you to pour the lemonade into the punch bowl. To stop it fizzing too much, try to pour it slowly down the inside of the bowl instead of sloshing it straight in.

* Add the cranberry juice and rosewater and stir gently.

* Carefully add the lime slices, raspberries, and mint leaves; they will float on the surface. **Ask a grown-up** to lift the bowl into the fridge until you want to serve it. But don't make it too far ahead of time or the lemonade will go flat.

* To serve, ladle the punch into glasses, making sure everyone gets some of the lime, raspberries, and mint leaves.

* *Serves 6 glasses of punch*

Ingredients you'll need
4¼ cups lemonade
2 cups cranberry juice
2 teaspoons rosewater
1 lime, thinly sliced
½ carton of raspberries
6 fresh, unblemished mint leaves

Equipment you'll need

measuring jug

measuring spoons

sharp knife and chopping board

2 quart capacity punch bowl, preferably clear

ladle (one with a lip is ideal)

75

Star-shaped rice fritters

These fritters are a great way to use up leftover rice. My mum used to make round fritters, but I think the star shapes look lovely.

Ingredients you'll need

2 cups cooked short-grain white rice
5 tablespoons 1 teaspoon all-purpose flour
2 eggs
⅓ cup orange juice
1 tablespoon 1 teaspoon vanilla-bean paste
1 tablespoon 1 teaspoon grated orange zest
2 teaspoons grated lemon zest
⅓ cup vegetable oil plus a little for greasing
2 tablespoons granulated sugar

Equipment you'll need

mixing bowls

whisk

measuring spoons

measuring cups

large metal kitchen spoon

pastry brush

frying pan

egg flip

citrus squeezer

4 star-shaped pancake rings (optional)

paper towels

zester

* Combine the rice and flour in a mixing bowl.

* Combine the eggs, orange juice, vanilla, and orange and lemon zests in another bowl and whisk them together well. **Ask a grown-up** to help you pour this egg mixture onto the rice and stir until well combined.

* Add the oil to the frying pan and **ask a grown-up** to help you heat it over a low heat.

* While the pan is heating, brush a little more oil inside the pancake rings. Put the pancake rings into the pan and allow them to heat for 1 minute.

* **Ask a grown-up** to help you spoon some of the rice batter into each pancake ring, filling them about halfway full. If you don't have pancake rings, just dollop a spoonful of the batter directly into the pan so that it forms a round pancake. Cook for 1 minute then use an egg flip to gently hold the fritter in place while lifting the pancake ring up and away from the pancake. **Ask a grown-up** to help you with this.

* **Ask a grown-up** to help you turn the fritters over and cook them for another minute on the other side. Lift the fritters out of the pan onto a paper towel to drain. Cook the rest of the batter to make more fritters.

* Lift the fritters onto a warm serving platter and sprinkle with granulated sugar before serving.

* *Makes around 8 fritters*

Raspberry delight

You could use strawberries for this dessert instead of raspberries if you prefer; just remember to take out the stalky bits and cut them in half if they are very big.

* **Ask a grown-up** to help you put the cream and vanilla bean paste into the bowl of an electric mixer. Beat until it thickens enough to form soft peaks when you lift out the beater.

* Pour half the raspberries into a small bowl and mash them with the sugar until it forms a smooth, runny sauce.

* Arrange a layer of cream in pretty glasses, then spoon a layer of raspberry sauce and then the raspberries. Repeat. Top each with 2 mint leaves and an extra raspberry.

* *Makes 4 desserts*

Tip
* It's a good idea to use raspberries as soon as you can after buying them, and certainly within 2 days.

Ingredients you'll need
1¼ cups cream
1 teaspoon vanilla-bean paste
2 cartons of raspberries
2 teaspoons granulated sugar
8 unblemished mint leaves

Equipment you'll need

potato masher

electric mixer

large metal kitchen spoon

large and small bowls

measuring spoons

4 pretty glass dessert bowls or glasses (around 2 in x 3 in)

Fun-shaped pancakes

My favorite pancake shapes are in the form of a boy and girl. They look so cute that they are almost too good to eat!

Ingredients you'll need

1 cup all-purpose flour
½ teaspoon baking soda
½ teaspoon baking powder
1 egg
¾ cup milk
½ teaspoon white vinegar
2 teaspoons softened butter
juice of 1 large lemon
3-4 tablespoons confectioners sugar for dusting

Equipment you'll need

whisk

sifter

measuring spoons

measuring cups

pastry brush

mixing bowls

egg flip

frying pan

lemon juicer

confectioners sugar shaker

novelty pancake rings (optional)

* Sift the flour, baking soda, and baking powder into a mixing bowl.

* Combine the egg, milk, and vinegar in another bowl and whisk them together well. **Ask a grown-up** to help you pour the egg mixture onto the dry ingredients and whisk them together.

* Add 1 teaspoon of the softened butter to the frying pan and use a pastry brush to grease it evenly. Brush a little more butter inside the pancake rings.

* **Ask a grown-up** to help you put the frying pan over a low heat and put the pancake rings in. Allow them to heat for 1 minute. Pour ¼ cup of batter into each ring so they are about a third full. If you're not using pancake rings then just pour the batter directly into the pan so that it forms a round pancake. Cook until bubbles start to appear on the surface, then use an egg flip to gently hold the pancake in place while lifting the pancake ring up and away from the pancake. **Ask a grown-up** to help you with this. Continue cooking for another minute, or until the pancake is cooked on the underside (lift the edge up with an egg flip and have a peek).

* **Ask a grown-up** to help you flip the pancakes over and cook them for 1–2 minutes on the other side, then lift out of the pan onto a warm plate. Cook the rest of the batter to make more pancakes.

* Serve the pancakes hot from the pan, sprinkled with lemon juice and confectioners sugar.

* *Makes 4 large pancakes*

Cute pancake shapes—almost too good to eat!

Vanilla rice pudding

Sometimes rice pudding is made in the oven. This one is made on the stove top in the same way as a risotto. This means you can use milk, instead of cream, which is fatty. The rice becomes really rich and creamy as it cooks.

* Combine the milk, vanilla, and sugar in a saucepan and **ask a grown-up** to help you heat it over a low–medium heat. Stir with a wooden spoon to help the sugar dissolve. It is a good idea to wear oven mitts while you do this to protect you from hot steam. When small bubbles start to appear, **ask a grown-up** to take over as hot milk can bubble up and boil over very quickly. Once the milk reaches boiling point turn the heat down to a very gentle simmer.

* Put the rice into another heavy-based saucepan and **ask a grown-up** to help you put it over a low–medium heat. Add a ladle of the simmering milk, again with a grown-up helping. Stir until the rice has absorbed all the milk, and as soon as it has, add another ladle of hot milk. Continue until all the milk is used up, making sure each ladle is fully absorbed before adding the next.

* Keep stirring the rice as the milk is added. This stops it sticking to the bottom of the pan and also helps the rice to break down into the milk and become lovely and thick and creamy. It will take about 30 minutes of cooking and stirring for the rice to become tender but still "al dente."*
As soon as it is cooked, turn off the heat and let it cool a little.

* **Ask a grown-up** to help you lightly roast the slivered almonds in a dry frying pan. Leave to cool a little.

* Spoon the rice pudding into 4 serving bowls and decorate with the roasted almonds.

* *Makes 4 servings of rice pudding*

  * "Al dente" means "tender to the bite" in Italian. "Al dente" rice feels
    soft when you bite it but is still firm and holds its shape.

Ingredients you'll need
4¼ cups milk
1 teaspoon vanilla-bean paste
2 tablespoons 2 teaspoons raw sugar
½ cup vialano nano or arborio rice
¼ cup slivered almonds

Equipment you'll need

measuring spoons   measuring jug

small saucepan and medium heavy-based saucepan

wooden spoon

measuring cups

frying pan   oven mitts   ladle

Thick-cut French toast

You can turn French toast into a really fancy breakfast by topping it with poached fruits, a dollop of whipped cream, and a drizzle of honey.

Ingredients you'll need

2 tablespoons raw sugar
½ teaspoon ground cinnamon
3 eggs
½ cup milk
4 x ¾ in slices casalinga (Italian crusty bread)
2 tablespoons 2 teaspoons vegetable oil for frying

Equipment you'll need

whisk
mixing bowls
measuring spoons
measuring cups
frying pan
tongs
egg flip
oven mitts

* Mix the sugar with the cinnamon in a small bowl.

* Combine the eggs and the milk in a medium mixing bowl and whisk them together well.

* Dunk the bread slices into the egg mixture, 2 at a time, and let them soak for about a minute on each side.

* While the bread is soaking, **ask a grown-up** to help you heat 1 table-spoon of the oil in a frying pan over a medium–high heat. Using tongs, lift the bread out of the egg mixture and place them in the frying pan. It's a good idea to wear oven mitts while you do this to protect you from any splashes of hot oil.

* Reduce the heat to low–medium and cook for 2–3 minutes on each side. To test that the French toast is cooked, press down on it with an egg flip to check that no runny egg comes out.

* **Ask a grown-up** to help you lift the French toast onto a warm serving platter and sprinkle over some of the cinnamon sugar. Repeat with the remaining slices of bread and serve immediately.

* *Makes 4 slices*

Little sticky date puddings

The butterscotch sauce recipe makes about ⅓ cup, so if you really love butterscotch, you could double the quantities.

* **Ask a grown-up** to help you preheat the oven to 320°F and grease the ramekin dishes with the butter.

* Combine the dates and water in a small saucepan. **Ask a grown-up** to heat it over a low heat and bring it to a boil. Turn off the heat.

* Add the baking soda to the dates (and watch it fizz!)**.** Stir well then leave to cool.

* Put the butter and sugar in the bowl of an electric mixer and beat until it looks pale and fluffy. Add the egg and beat until it is well combined.

* Sift the flour into a mixing bowl then add half of it to the beaten egg mixture. Use a large kitchen spoon to stir them together, working from the middle of the bowl. Instead of stirring round and round, try to cut downwards through the mixture and then turn it over (this is called "folding"). When the flour is folded in, add half of the cooled date mixture and fold that in. Repeat with the rest of the flour and then the rest of the date mixture.

* Divide the pudding mixture between the ramekin dishes, then put them on a cookie sheet and **ask a grown-up** to help you put it in the oven on the middle shelf. Cook for 25 minutes or until cooked through. The puddings are done when a skewer inserted into the middle comes out cleanly.

* While the puddings are cooking, make the butterscotch sauce. Combine the ingredients in a saucepan and **ask a grown-up** to help you heat it over a low–medium heat. Stir everything gently until the butter and cream have melted and the sugar has dissolved. It is a good idea to wear oven mitts while you do this to protect your hands from any hot splashes. Let the sauce boil gently for 1 minute.

* **Ask a grown-up** to take the puddings out of the oven and to help you unmould them onto dessert plates. Use a small spatula to loosen the edges—the puddings should come out cleanly. Spoon some of the butterscotch sauce over the top of each pudding and serve right away.

* *Makes 4 small puddings*

Ingredients you'll need
½ teaspoon butter for greasing
½ cup pitted dates
1 cup water
1 teaspoon baking soda
3¾ tablespoons softened butter
¼ cup raw sugar
1 egg
½ cup self-rising flour

BUTTERSCOTCH SAUCE
4 tablespoons butter
¼ cup cream
½ cup brown sugar
½ teaspoon vanilla-bean paste

Equipment you'll need

measuring spoons

measuring cups

4 ramekin dishes
(3½ in × 1½ in)

saucepans

wooden spoon

electric mixer

small spatula

large metal kitchen spoon

metal skewer

sifter

cookie sheet

oven mitts

mixing bowls

Chocolate pudding

Most people love chocolate and this pudding is excellent because it magically makes its own sauce as it cooks.

Ingredients you'll need

1 teaspoon butter for greasing
¼ cup walnuts
½ cup all-purpose flour
4 tablespoons granulated sugar
1 teaspoon baking powder
1 pinch of salt
2 tablespoons 2 teaspoons cocoa
2¾ tablespoons butter
¼ cup milk
½ teaspoon vanilla-bean paste
1 egg
whipped cream to serve (optional)

TOPPING
1 cup brown sugar
2 tablespoons 2 teaspoons cocoa
1 cup boiling water

Equipment you'll need

mortar and pestle
mixing bowls
13½ oz baking dish
wooden spoon
sifter
whisk
measuring spoons
measuring cups
saucepan

* **Ask a grown-up** to help you preheat the oven to 320°F and grease baking dish with the butter.

* Use a mortar and pestle to roughly crush the walnuts, then pour them into a large mixing bowl.

* Sift the flour onto the walnuts and add the granulated sugar, baking powder, salt, and cocoa. Stir everything around so it is mixed together well.

* Place the butter in a saucepan and **ask a grown-up** to help you melt it over a low heat. Pour it into another mixing bowl and add the vanilla and the egg. Quickly whisk everything together well.

* Pour into the dry ingredients and stir everything together gently, then **ask a grown-up** to help you scrape the batter into the baking dish.

* To make the topping, mix the brown sugar with the cocoa and sprinkle it over the top of the pudding. **Ask a grown-up** to measure out the boiling water and pour it slowly over the top of the pudding. Place in the oven and bake for 30 minutes or until it is risen and firm to the touch.

* **Ask a grown-up** to help you take the pudding out of the oven and serve it immediately with whipped cream if you like.

* *Serves 6*

Drumroll please . . .

To my husband Anthony, who has been there from the start; I owe him everything.

To Maria, my mum, and my two nonnas, Carmela and Lilliana, who cooked interesting meals all the time when I was younger and who let me watch, experiment, and most importantly, taste their creations. What a revelation it was, being allowed to watch fresh pasta hanging out to dry, tomato sauce being bottled, bread emerging from a wood-fired oven, and having a dedicated dessert-making table at Christmas.

To my eternally-kind dad who will do anything for anyone. He believed in me and Little Kitchen before anyone else did.

To my very cute younger brother and sister, J-Man (James) and Missy (Mia) for cooking with me onstage and off.

To my staff, the "A Team": Chrissie Atkinson, Maria Boeddu, Jo Jolly, Lisa Luscombe, Lisa Miatke, Steph Perin, Rachel Sands, Madi Turner. You are a gorgeous bunch who make Little Kitchen run like clockwork and I am truly indebted.

Big thanks also to Rachel, who is one of the most amazing chefs I've seen in action. Our students love her and with good reason. Rachel contributed some excellent family favorites for us to at our cookery school and I'm delighted to be able to include them in the book.

Extra special thanks go to Lisa M. (one of the most awe-inspiring early childhood educators I've met), for helping me with this book during our holiday break. She proof-read, made lots of excellent suggestions, and helped put the finishing touches on the recipes. She's a real gem.

To the many friends and family members who have cooked meals for me, thanks for inspiring so many of the recipes in this book.

Thanks to everyone at Hardie Grant Books for offering me this delicious opportunity. It has been one of my most enjoyable and tasty adventures to date! In particular, heartfelt thanks to my publisher Mary Small, managing editor Ellie Smith, to photographer Jacqui Melville, designer Trisha Garner, and editor Lucy Malouf.

And finally, to the thousands of Little Kitchen customers over the years, thanks for supporting our school and for allowing your children to teach us. Your positive word-of-mouth recommendations have ensured we've been able to grow, improve our program, and offer an amazing experience for everyone who walks through the door.

Sabrina Parrini

Sabrina Parrini was fortunate to start her cooking adventures as a very young child. In fact, one of her earliest and fondest memories is of cooking gnocchi alfresco in her grandmother's backyard overlooking the veggie garden and wood-fired oven. As a child, Sabrina's family were huge advocates of growing their own food, home-style cooking, and eating well. Growing up in an environment where food played such a vital role, Sabrina continued to cook and learn under the tutelage of her mother (a great home cook) and is now a grown-up with an unswerving passion for cooking and enjoying good, tasty food.

It was in the classroom kitchen, when she was working as an early childhood teacher, that Sabrina became inspired to start her initiative, Little Kitchen, and teach more children about the importance of cooking and eating good food. Sabrina saw how much "natural" learning was taking place in the kitchen. In addition, cooking was an activity that didn't distinguish between girls and boys and both sexes would excitedly race to the kitchen counter as soon as cooking time was announced.

Many years later Sabrina established her child-inspired cookware range and her children's cookery center to continue to nurture the enthusiasm displayed by her little students in her preschool kitchen.

All these cooking adventures have led Sabrina to pull together all her favorite recipes from Little Kitchen and present them in this fun and friendly book.